fit not fat

The
**Ultimate
Asian Diet Plan**
with recipes to achieve
your ideal weight!

Anna Jacob & Ng Hooi Lin

Marshall Cavendish
Cuisine

Editor: Lydia Leong
Designer: Steven Tan
Photographer: Joshua Tan, Elements By the Box

Published by Marshall Cavendish Cuisine
An imprint of Marshall Cavendish International
1 New Industrial Road, Singapore 536196

Other Marshall Cavendish Offices:

Marshall Cavendish International. PO Box 65829 London EC1P 1NY, UK
• Marshall Cavendish Corporation. 99 White Plains Road, Tarrytown NY
10591-9001, USA • Marshall Cavendish International (Thailand) Co Ltd.
253 Asoke, 12th Flr, Sukhumvit 21 Road, Klongtoey Nua, Wattana, Bangkok
10110, Thailand • Marshall Cavendish (Malaysia) Sdn Bhd, Times Subang,
Lot 46, Subang Hi-Tech Industrial Park, Batu Tiga, 40000 Shah Alam,
Selangor Darul Ehsan, Malaysia

Marshall Cavendish is a trademark of Times Publishing Limited

National Library Board, Singapore Cataloguing-in-Publication Data

Jacob, Anna,- 1962-
Fit not fat : the ultimate Asian diet plan with recipes to achieve your ideal
weight in weeks! /- Anna Jacob & Ng Hooi Lin. – Singapore : Marshall
Cavendish Cuisine, c2010.
p. cm.
ISBN-13 : 978-981-4276-66-5

1. Reducing diets- – Recipes. 2. Low-fat diet- – Recipes. 3. Low-calorie diet-
– Recipes. 4. Reducing diets- – Asia. I. Ng, Hooi Lin.
II. Title.

TX714
641.5635 -- dc22   OCN657024562

Printed in Singapore by KWF Printing Pte Ltd

Dedication

We would to thank all the wonderful people who made this book possible.

Lydia Leong, our editor. Thank you for believing in us and giving us this opportunity to give of our best knowledge and skills to help individuals achieve and maintain a healthy weight through life.

We also want to thank Steven Tan for patiently bearing with our wishes and making this book a visual delight.

The Lord Jesus. I can do nothing except that You bless, guide and support me.

My husband, Jibby Jacob, for the space and support you've given me for every creative endeavour. I cannot begin to express my love and gratitude.

My daughter, Divya Susan Jacob. You are truly my inspiration to reach for the stars.

My mother, Elizabeth Abraham. You are my anchor through the ups and downs of life.

Ng Hooi Lin. You have been a great colleague and an inspiring friend.

Myrna Partible. Thank you for allowing us to mess up the kitchen day after day.

Anna Jacob

My mother, Koh Koon Qui and my sisters, Hooi Chueen and Yuen Choo, for filling my life with so much love and joy.

Anna Jacob for inviting me to work on this book.

My good friends, Wong Chen Siang, Christina Ng, Ng Boon Huat, Chang Wei Fung and Zhang Qinghua, for being an important part of my life, inspiring and supporting me all the time.

My blog readers, for your support and encouragement.

Myra Partible, for teaching me to cook from scratch.

Ng Hooi Lin

Contents

Preface

Flip a few magazines or turn on the telly and you will see trim and well-toned models, actors and actresses traipsing across the pages and the tube. Yet, health authorities bemoan the rising number of obese individuals in many nations. It is true. More and more of us struggle to achieve and maintain an appropriate weight for height. And, if you have picked up this book, it's probably because either you or a loved one is struggling with a weight issue.

The extra kilos that you may carry not only contributes to an unflattering change in shape, they bring along a host of daily discomforts and raise the risk for lifestyle-related diseases. Simple daily tasks—walking, working and bending—are tougher. The heart, lungs and joints work harder to carry the load and wear out faster. Over and above that, the extra weight per se is a risk factor for raising blood fat and sugar levels and building up pressure in the arteries which in turn increase your risk of heart diseases. All in all, being overweight puts a damper on the quality of your life and shortens your lifespan.

So, what does the future hold for you and me? Living in an environment that is energy efficient and abundant in delicious food, we are set to let the kilos pile on. To survive this real-life threat, we need to work to attain and maintain an appropriate weight throughout life.

The keys to weigh in right always are: awareness, knowledge and a practical plan to eat less and exercise more. This behaviour change must last a lifetime.

If you are ready to improve your eating style to get from fat to fit, this book will provide a valuable guide. Practical information, meal plans and lower Calorie Asian recipes will help you to continue to enjoy eating while cutting back on fat, sugar and food portions effectively. For sustained success, your nutrition 'makeover' must be coupled with regular and effective exercise.

Weight loss is hard work. And keeping the weight off is even harder. Focus on one small lifestyle change at a time. Once it becomes a habit, add on one more. Soon, you will celebrate your fit figure and new lease on life.

Here's to your best health! Get set to weigh in right!

Anna Jacob & Ng Hooi Lin

Introduction

"*You've lost some weight, Anna, and you look great! How did you do it?*"

> "*Yes, Hooi Lin. I've lost over 6 kg in the last 6 months. Careful eating and regular exercise helped me shed the extra weight I was carrying.*"

"*Was it difficult to achieve your weight loss? What inspired you?*"

> "*Yes, it was a long and hard journey that required focused attention and perseverance. Actually, the possibility of writing this book inspired me.*"

"*What were your challenges? How did you overcome them?*"

> "*I love food and I love to laze around. I needed to give up my 'fat-mindset' and develop a 'fit mind-set'. I had to overcome my fears and inhibitions to learn and adopt a healthier living plan. Can you believe it? I used to fear eating less as I thought I would get hungry. I thought I would not be able to resist my craving to indulge in treat foods like ice cream and cakes! I had to get off the couch and find a way to fit regular exercise into my work day. Having a gym near my workplace worked for me. I never ever saw myself as the 'gymming-type', but it was doable and so, it worked.*"

"Great job! Now that you have achieved a healthier weight, focus on health goals and keep going! The weight loss will stay off for life."

"Thanks Hooi Lin, but I worry that the weight will creep back on. But I also remember that you once told me that if I wanted something badly enough, I can work hard to get it."

"Yes, motivation is the key to help you keep the weight off. Have you ever thought of getting your family involved?"

"Yes, they are involved! Watching me has inspired my husband to take to the gym too and he has lost quite a few kilos as well! And, my daughter, with her medical training, ensures that we both approach weight loss in a safe and sensible manner. What about you? What are your weight challenges?"

"I need to work hard to keep my weight up. I love to cycle and run half marathons, so my challenge is to eat enough."

"That's a 'happy-problem'. You get to eat a lot more. But, remember to eat healthfully too."

"I will. Now, we can truly share some practical and effective tips on weight management with those who are serious about losing their extra weight or maintaining their ideal weight!"

On Your Mark...

Like any good race, you have to get started. Desire for weight loss must translate into specific actions that set you up to succeed.

Are You Ready?

Take this simple 5-point test to see how likely you are to succeed at shedding and keeping off the kilos.

1 Compared with all previous attempts at weight loss, how much more motivated are you this time?

0 --------- 1 --------- 2 --------- 3 --------- 4 --------- 5

Not motivated   Very motivated

2 How willing are you to eat less food?

0 --------- 1 --------- 2 --------- 3 --------- 4 --------- 5

Not willing   Very willing

3 How willing are you to cut back on food that contains a lot of fat and sugar?

0 --------- 1 --------- 2 --------- 3 --------- 4 --------- 5

Not willing   Very willing

4 Are you prepared to exercise for at least 30 minutes everyday (or at least 5 times a week)?

0 --------- 1 --------- 2 --------- 3 --------- 4 --------- 5

Not prepared   Very prepared

5 Are you willing to sustain your new lifestyle goals?

0 --------- 1 --------- 2 --------- 3 --------- 4 --------- 5

No   Yes

What Your Score Reveals

20–25

You are revved up sufficiently to get started and keep going.
Keep tracking your goals to stay engaged.

10–19

You are fairly likely to succeed. Build in incentives and engage
supportive people to encourage you on.

<10

You are not ready for the rigor of the weight loss journey. Revisit
the reasons why you thought you wanted to try to shed some weight.
Learn more about why you need to do just that. Enlist professional
and family support to get you more excited about getting fitter.

Weigh In

Stand on the weighing scale at least once a week. Weight is a simple and effective health measure that you can track with ease. Being under or overweight for your height is a risk factor for certain diseases. So track and analyse your weight regularly. Discuss any drastic weight change you note with your physician.

Measure Up

Get a measuring tape—a simple tailoring one will do. Measure your waist circumference and record it. Every week, pull out the tape and repeat the measurement. As you lose weight, your waist circumference should drop too.

Fat or Fit?

Weight

Some measure it in kilogrammes and others prefer pounds. Weight per se is just a number. Use the Body Mass Index (BMI) ratio to interpret the impact that your weight may have on your future health.

> **Fact**
>
> 1 kilogramme (kg)
> = 2.2 pounds (lb)

You may already know that being either underweight or overweight increases your risk of developing chronic, lifestyle related diseases.

$$\text{Body Mass Index (BMI)} = \frac{\text{Weight (kg)}}{\text{Height (m) x Height (m)}}$$

What your BMI means

< 18.5	: Underweight
18.5–22.9	: Normal weight
23.0–27.4	: Overweight
27.5 and above	: Very overweight

Waist Dimensions

You may wonder why we choose to focus on the fat at the waist. Studies have shown that abdominal weight is abominable! Fat pads over the tummy elevate blood fat levels far more than fat tucked away over the bottom or on your arms. As you succeed at shedding the kilos, the fat deposits should also be worked off. So do not be satisfied with weight loss that is mostly water loss!

Extremely low carb diets and wraps and saunas tend to dehydrate you. Of course you are impressed by the immediate shift in the scale but think about it, you have just lost a lot of water! Drink a glass of water and you will see the lever moving up again.

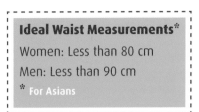

Ideal Waist Measurements*

Women: Less than 80 cm

Men: Less than 90 cm

* For Asians

Set Your Fit Weight Goal

If your BMI is higher or lower than recommended, you need to set a weight goal that will help you get fitter. Good management rule books suggest setting SMART goals that are Specific, Measureable, Achievable, Realistic and with a Time frame.

A weight loss of 0.5 kg to 1 kg per week is usually recommended. Anything lower will make the process a drag. A higher goal is hard to achieve. Use the Weight Loss Planner (page 14) to chart out your goal.

The Right Weigh

Weigh yourself...

- Just once a week
- On the same weighing scale
- In similar clothing
- At about the same time, preferably before breakfast, after the early morning visit to the loo

Track Your Progress

Weight loss is a journey—and a hard one! You need to work at it over a period of time—shorter for those who have just a few kilos to get rid off and longer for those who have more weight to lose. It is important to chart the journey or you are likely to go off course mid-way through. Here are some tips to keep you going.

- Plan your weight loss, specify actual weight goal and time frame.
- Apart from weight, include other fitness goals. For example, increase the duration of the jog; raise the incline on the treadmill; push up the speed.
- Build in incentives along the way to celebrate each success. Make sure they are non-food related.

Weight Loss Planner

		Week 1 Date _____	Week 2 Date _____
My Plan	My goal weight (kg) (Aim for 0.5–1 kg weight loss per week)		
	My fitness goals		
	My incentive plan		
My Achievements	Actual weight (kg)		
	Waist circumference (cm)		
	Fitness goal achieved (Yes / No)		
	Incentives achieved (Yes / No)		

Week 3 Date _____	Week 4 Date _____	Week 5 Date _____	Week ____ Date _____

Get Set. . .

Every journey takes preparation for success. Take a quick rain check on your knowledge about weight loss. Evaluate what you have gathered against good science with the help of your physician or nutritionist. With the right know-how, you are more likely to get to your goal with fewer hindrances.

Myths & Misperceptions

I need a 'special diet' to succeed

Many vouch for the 'new-diet' printed off the Internet or championed by a friend's friend. Here is a sampler of some diet fads.

Carb free

This one has had its time in the sun. Somehow carbs are easy to hate. Keeping carb intake below 100 g per day, triggers breakdown of fat and protein to create 'ketones'—an alternate fuel that keeps the brain powered. The body washes out these toxic molecules as fast as it can, dehydrating the body and lightening the scales quite dramatically. But once carbs and water are replaced in the diet, the scales will trend up.

Soup diet

Soups are generally low in Calories unless laced with fat and cream (think seafood gumbo or cream of asparagus soup). Filling up on low Calorie cabbage soup or spinach soup or celery soup displaces solid from the diet and leads to weight loss. Sustaining this soupy foods diet over time is hard and fraught with the risk of developing nutritional deficiencies.

Juice diet

Harmless as this seems, fruit juices are quite energy-dense or Caloric. Over consumption of fruit juices can lead to weight gain and not weight loss. Like the soup diet, apart from malnutrition, the side effects include boredom and many trips to the loo.

High protein

Before you salivate about the large steaks you can eat without any guilt, know that the term is relative. New studies have shown that low Calorie diets that are marginally higher in protein than regular diets, are satiating and likely to cause weight loss more effectively than higher carb diets. But extremely high protein diets, anchored in animal proteins like meat, poultry, eggs and more, tend to be high in saturated fat and cholesterol, all of which work together to block up arteries.

So, before you seek the thrills and spills of another new diet, know that a well-balanced diet made up of grains, proteins, dairy, fruit and vegetables is the best foundation even for a lower Calorie diet.

I need to 'detox' to shed weight

The human body is robust. It is designed by nature to get rid of waste. Pooing, peeing and sweating are the natural forms of detoxification. Weight fluctuations due to constipation may add a kilo or two. For individuals in good health, all one has to do is get adequate fibre and fluid to enjoy regular bowel habits. If you are stressing about water retention, you must know that the adult human body is more than 60 per cent water. If you really feel you are retaining fluids, see your physician as soon as possible for a review of your kidney function. With normally functioning kidneys, you can remove any additional water effectively. If anyone is promising weight loss by dehydrating you, wise up.

I need slimming pills to shed stubborn fats

Slimming pills come in a great variety. Some are just hocus pocus but others are based on clinical evidence from good scientific trials. Your physician is your best resource to discuss this question and to advice you on your need for pills that may help you feel fuller faster, curb your appetite or prevent you from absorbing nutrients. But all of them will work much better if you pay attention to your eating and exercise plans. In fact you must, as you do not want to be dependent on these drugs for the rest of your life.

I can succeed with meal replacements

It is logical, yes, you can. If you replace a meal that is higher in Calories with a meal replacement that is lower in Calories and keep going for a while, you will lose weight. But you need to use the right meal replacement in the right way. Well designed, nutritionally complete meal replacements are useful for those who need to lose weight in a hurry for medical purposes such as preparing for a surgery or for those who cannot and will not improve their eating habits. However, if you choose to go this route, speak with your physician and get the support of a nutritionist or dietitian to help you design a suitable plan. But remember, meal replacements come with fewer flavours and textures than real foods and may therefore become a bit hard to adhere to.

The ABCs of Weight Loss

All About Calories

Over the next few weeks and months and maybe, years as you focus on getting your weight down, you will need to become familiar with the Calorie.

The Calorie (Cal or kcal) is just a unit of measurement for the energy contained in food and the energy used up for living and activity.

Food Calories

Nature locks away 'energy' into the carbohydrate, protein and fat molecules in food. Vitamins and minerals are not true sources of energy. But like 'sparks', some of them play vital roles in releasing energy from the 'power-packed' nutrients that the body combusts.

Heart-friendly fats

All fats deliver the same Calories but some are more heart-friendly, for example, monounsaturated fats such as canola, peanut and olive oils. You can also use small portions of polyunsaturated fats such as soy, corn, sunflower and safflower oils.

Lean proteins

While protein and carbs look on par, most protein choices such as chicken, fish, meat and milk naturally contain some fat. So go lean or low fat on your choices.

Carb—a low Calorie option

Carbs are often eaten plain in many parts of Asia (remember that plain rice, *ketupat*, *mantou* and *suka roti* are traditional carb-rich options that are totally acceptable as the staple in the diet) and so may be the lowest Calorie nutrient option. Surprised? Well, as long as you do not eat a mountain of it, carbs per se are not fattening.

Did You Know?

Fat packs away more than double the energy held in either a protein or carbohydrate molecule. So one of the most easy and effective ways to cut back on Calories is to degrease your diet.

The Caloric Trio

Fat   : 9 Calories per gramme
Protein   : 4 Calories per gramme
Carbohydrate : 4 Calories per gramme

Special carbs

High fibre and lower GI carbs are digested slower than refined carbs and so they trigger a lower demand for insulin—the hormone charged with helping the body lower blood sugar. One of the many ways that insulin does that is to convert sugar to fat. So these special carbs may help you store away less fat in your reserves.

Activity Calories

It takes energy, that is, Calories to stay alive. Just staying powered up—keeping your breath going, your heart beating and your gut digesting the food you ate a while ago, you need Calories. Thinking, walking, working, playing—and all the other things you do each day demands Calories too. The more intense an activity is, the longer you do it and the more muscle you use to do it—the more power it drains from your system too. Refer to the Calorie Expenditure Table (page 178) for the estimated number of Calories burned while doing various activities.

To lose weight, you need to reduce the time you spend in sedentary activities such as watching television, surfing the Internet or staying glued to your work desk. The time saved is best spent in active exercise.

If you wonder which exercise is best, know that while the scientists debate on the theories, you may just want to get off the couch and do something today. And, when you have made exercise a regular part of your life, increase the intensity and the duration to raise the Caloric deficit you need for the weight to wear off.

Ideally, you do need a combination of exercise types to burn off the Calories effectively and build up your lean body mass. A lean, mean and fit body machine expends Calories more effectively and for longer than a fat-laden one.

High Fibre Carbs

- Brown rice
- Wholemeal bread
- Wholemeal pasta
- Brown rice vermicelli
- Wholemeal biscuits
- Beans

Lower GI Carbs

- Pearl barley
- Soba noodles
- Basmati rice
- Sweet potato
- Sweet corn
- Carrot
- Grapefruit
- Apple
- Orange
- Banana
- Kiwi fruit

Heart-friendly work out

Using the larger muscle groups such as your legs and arms demands more Calories and oxygen. Brisk walking, jogging, cycling and swimming are examples of these energy-drainers. So pick any one and get started. Keep at it and you will soon enjoy the rush of blood and oxygen being pumped through your system.

> **Get the Lift**
>
> Here is a secret to share—a great work out releases 'happy-hormones' in your brain—the endorphins—and, they go a long way to making you feel great each day. In fact, you will want to come back to exercise each day for more!!

Resistance

Apart from losing weight and body fat, pick weight-bearing exercises that help build up your muscle mass. The more muscles you have (ladies, do not faint—you do not have to have a six-pack to benefit from this) the more energy you burn when you do any task. Light weights and bench presses are weight bearing exercises that will make you stronger over time.

Start Right, Stay Safe

- If you have not been exercising for a while, check with your physician to be sure that you are fit enough to start on a regime. You may even want to work with a personal trainer to help you start at your own pace and build up as you get stronger.

- Wear lose and comfortable clothing.

- Ensure that you are well hydrated before, during and after exercise.

- Always remember to warm up before you revv up your body machine.

- Start slowly. You are not in competition with any one.

- Start at 40 per cent of your maximum heart rate (MHR) for the first 4–5 weeks for 12–20 minutes. Then progress up to 70 per cent of the MHR over time. Always exercise just hard enough to break a sweat and yet, be able to maintain a conversation.

> **Work out your Maximum Heart Rate (MHR)**
>
> MHR = 220 – Age (years)

- Keep going. Slow and steady wins the race.

- Listen to your body. While it is natural to feel some aches and pains when you start, if it is more intense than usual, take a day off. But get back to your exercise regime as fast as possible. Stay away for too long and you will go through starting pains again.

- As you get lighter and fitter, increase the duration and intensity of your exercise programme. But do so slowly.

- Do not exercise when you have fever, cough or cold.

How Much Can I Eat Each Day?

There are many ways to answer this question. The best answer is one that suits your personality, so pick the one that suits your style:

I look for the big picture. I hate details.

Read The Survivor's Guide (page 23).

I like details and I deal well with numbers.

Read The Calorie Counter's Guide (page 26).

I can deal with the big picture and the small details.

Read both The Survivor's Guide (page 23) and The Calorie Counter's Guide (page 26).

The Survivor's Guide

There are just three simple weight-losing diet tips you need to know.

1 Degrease Your Diet

Fat is the focus. While there are good fats—the fats that are heart healthy and immune-enhancing - we need them in very small quantities. All the extra fat we take is to please our 'fat-tooth'— because fat is an amazing source of flavour and aroma molecules and, it also improves mouth-feel too. No wonder fat-rich foods taste good and we go back for more and more. You have got to overcome this 'pull' to degrease your diet.

Review your diet and pick out the areas where fat has crept in. Fat is insidious. You will need to be discerning.

- Choose low fat foods. Look for labels that highlight the Healthier Choice Symbol as they are the relatively better choice in that category of food. (The Healthier Choice Symbol is a national programme run by the Health Promotion Board in Singapore to help the public identify healthier food in the supermarket.)

- Use less oil or fat when you prepare foods. Get out the nonstick pan or use a cooking spray if you want to stir-fry or pan-fry food. Alternately, steam, boil or grill to cook food without added fat.

- Avoid buying deep-fried and cream-laden cooked foods for snacks or main meals. Here's how:

  — Do the "look test" to discover fat-laden foods. Anything that glistens with oil or has a layer of oil and cream floating over it probably has a lot more fat than is good for you.

  — Do the "press test". Take a kitchen towel or a paper napkin. Place the suspect food on it and press it gently with the towel. If you see fat ooze with ease onto the sheets of papyrus, then, you have just identified a suspect fat food. Now, give it up! It does better lining the bin than your waist!

  — Do the "ask test". Ask the waiter, the hawker or the chef how the food is prepared. If you hear a lot about oil, cream or fat, you may want to ask for help to select a less fat-filled choice.

2 Slash the Added Sugars

Sugars are naturally present in fruit and milk. Starchy carbs like rice and noodles break down slowly in the body to yield sugars too. In these natural forms, sugar makes food taste good and brings with it many natural nutrients. However, with added sugars, one needs to exercise caution. While "just a spoonful of sugar makes the medicine (and, nutritious food) go down", in large portions, it bring along a large dose of 'empty Calories' that one can do without when you want to lose weight. So, use added sugars—table sugar, honey and plam sugar—in moderation. Just a tad to get the food to taste good, but not in large quantities such that it adds unwanted Calories to your diet.

Now, if you have a sweet tooth, you have over time developed a preference for intensely sweetened foods. Breaking this habit will take time. But the good news is that habits can be broken. Decrease the amount of sugar you use in your beverages and desserts, and slowly but steadily, over time, you will begin to enjoy the natural flavours of foods.

3 Cut Back on Portions

If you are overweight, it simply is because you ate more than you should for your lifestyle. To lose weight, eat less of everything. Here are some practical ways to do just this:

- Eat about 70 per cent of your usual portion.

- Put all that you should eat on a plate and do not go for seconds. Try using a smaller plate—the visual effect of a full albeit smaller plate gives the impression of more food and can help you feel satisfied even though you are eating less.

- Never ever eat until you feel full.

- Never let anyone force you into eating more.

- Any extras at the table can be stored away in the refrigerator, reheated and used on another day.

Greed vs. Need

Faced with a banquet of delicious food, you need to learn to eat just enough. Train your brain to recognise your eating cues. Learn to distinguish between eating to meet nutritional need and indulging.

Red Flags

You are eating because you are:

- Reveling in the flavour, aroma or texture of food
- Eating out of habit for example, it is time for lunch; snacking in front of the television; eating at gatherings
- Being clever—making it worth the money you spent
- Bored, hungry, angry or happy
- Afraid that you may get hungry later
- Pleasing others

Survivor Skills

Eat to live, never, live to eat. Here are some useful skills to stay trim.

- Eat only when you are hungry
- Select the most nutritious choices
- Serve your self your portion on a plate and eat only that quantity
- Do not go for seconds
- Do not snack unless you are hungry
- Walk away from the food when you have eaten your portion
- Never eat while you do other things such as watching television, or a movie

The Calorie Counter's Guide

All About Calories

Think about Calories as you would your salary. You would not go to work unless you know you what you were being paid. Likewise, you should not eat unless you know how much you can eat. So it makes good sense to know your Calorie allowance.

Your Calorie allowance sets your limit for the amount of food you can eat each day—not less and not more. However, unlike money, there is no value in saving Calories. Any extra consumed will plug into your fat depots. To shed weight and knock it off from the fat laden stores, you need to work out a deficit and here's where you can learn how to budget it in.

Calculate Your Calorie Allowance

There are many ways to do this, ranging from the accurate to the almost close enough methods. If you are on the weight loss journey, a rough and ready method is good enough. Multiply your bodyweight by 30. This would yield the number of Calories you can eat each day to maintain your current weight. But if you want to shed weight, you need to eat less than this.

Example

Today, Mrs Tan is 152 cm and 70 kg.
Mrs Tan needs (70 kg x 30 Calories) = 2100 Calories each day to stay at her current weight.

Calorie Allowance To Stay At My Present Weight

Today, I am _____ cm and _____ kg.

I need (_____ kg x 30 Calories) = _____ Calories

each day to stay at my current weight.

The Math of Weight Loss

Weight loss is not rocket science! All you have to do is know the following facts to work it out.

- A kilogramme of fat in the body stores up to 7000 Calories.
- To work a kilogramme off, you need to create a Calorie deficit over time.
- If you eat 500 Calories less each day, over a week, you can accumulate a Calorie deficit of 3,500 Calories.
- This would account for half a kilogramme of weight loss at the end of a week.

Now, if you have an exercise programme in place as well, you will shed more than the expected half a kilogramme each week.

With effective weight loss, you need to go at it like the wise tortoise—slow and steady wins this race. If you get at it like the speedy hare, you will be all excited at the start but you will not be able to sustain it.

Example

Today, Mrs Tan is 152 cm and 70 kg.
Mrs Tan needs (70 kg x 30 Calories) 2100 Calories each day to stay at her current weight. To shed half a kilogramme each week, Mrs Tan must eat (2100 - 500 Calories) = 1600 Calories each day.

Calorie Allowance To Shed Weight

To shed half a kilogramme each week,

I must eat (_____ – 500 Calories) = _____ Calories each day.

Using Your Calorie Allowance

Now, that you know how much you need to eat each day to reach your weight loss goal, mix and match foods to stay within the allowance. This book will provide a menu planner and recipes to help you count Calories. There is a 1200 Calorie per day Menu Planner (page 174) for smaller individuals and a 1500 Calorie per day Menu Planner (page 176) for those of us who start out with a heavier weight. In addition, read food labels and search the Internet for the Calorie values of common foods.

Example

Mrs Tan's Calorie Allowance is 1600 Calories each day.
Here's how she may spread it through the day:

Breakfast	Lunch	Snack	Dinner
300 Cal	500 Cal	300 Cal	500 Cal

Spread Your Calorie Allowance Through Meals and Snacks

Your Calorie Allowance for the Day: _____ Calories

Breakfast	Lunch	Snack	Dinner
____ Cal	____ Cal	____ Cal	____ Cal

Aim for Great Value

While you focus on Calories, remember to make up your meals and snacks with foods that are of great nutritional value. Every Calorie you eat should deliver vitamin, minerals and phytochemicals, that is, natural components in food that are beneficial to health. So focus on the best in every food category. Here's how:

Eat a Well-balanced Diet

No matter how far nutrition science of weight loss progresses, people relate best to food not nutrients. So make sure as your diet 'lightens' up on Calories, it should be rich in the vital nutrients that will help you stay optimally nourished. Do not compromise on quality. Include grain-foods—rice, noodles, pasta, bread, biscuits and buns; protein-rich foods—meat, poultry, fish, seafood, dried beans and legumes; milk and milk products—low fat yoghurt and cheese; fruit and vegetables in your diet every day. The Healthy Diet Pyramid (below) is a practical and simple tool to help you achieve this.

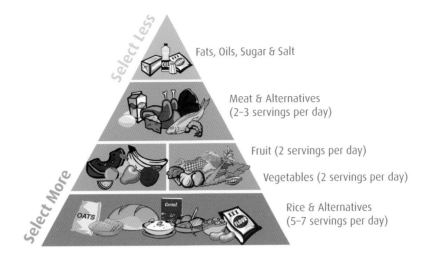

Select Less

Fats, Oils, Sugar & Salt

Meat & Alternatives
(2–3 servings per day)

Fruit (2 servings per day)

Vegetables (2 servings per day)

Select More

Rice & Alternatives
(5–7 servings per day)

Select the Most Wholesome Choices

In every food group, there are more wholesome choices. If you are one that likes a great bargain, then you should go for great value. The chart below shows you how.

Food Group	More Wholesome Choices
Rice & Alternatives	Wholegrain foods such as brown and red rice, brown rice vermicelli, wholemeal pasta, oats, wholemeal bread, wholemeal flour, wholemeal biscuits, corn kernels
Meat & Alternatives	Lean meat, skinless poultry (especially breast and thigh meat), naturally fatty fish (e.g. salmon, tuna and mackerel), dried beans and peas, soy foods such as soy bean curd and calcium-fortified soy milk, low fat or non-fat dairy products such as milk, yoghurt and cheese
Vegetables	Fresh vegetables
Fruit	Fresh and dried fruit

Go for Lower Fat, Lower Sugar and Lower Sodium Choices

Beyond weight loss, you should keep an eye on fat, added sugar and sodium as well. Used in small portions, they add flavour to the diet and are not detrimental to long-term health. However, if your choices are loaded with these flavour enhancers, then the quality of your diet dips. Changing taste preferences takes time but it can be done. Over time, the more natural and wholesome foods you eat will taste wonderful. But to get there, it will take concerted effort. Remember though that you need to get there for your overall health.

Go...

Now that you have all the information you need, you can start on your 'diet' programme! Think about it as your opportunity not just to lose weight but to get healthier too. You can make this journey a thrill or a drag—it is up to you!

The next few pages of this book will provide a menu planner for 1200 and 1500 Calories each day. These planners use many of the recipes in the book to help you enjoy a lower Calorie but nutrient-dense eating plan. Pick one and use it as your guide to get to your journey's end. Or, use it as a reference to build a meal plan of your own with some of the recipes in this book to lighten up your regular choices.

Journal Your Journey

What we eat, the exercise we do and the activities we undertake each day are really very personal and, sometimes, so much part of our life that we do not focus on it. Keeping a food and exercise journal along the weight loss journey will help you focus on it and focus on it long enough to see success. Some of us are old school and, we enjoy a hard copy. Others are more tech savvy and may like to keep a blog or maintain an electronic version. Any which way, just do it!

Review your journal often and, track your success or failure. Be honest, deadly honest— it is the simplest way to get to the root of the problem. If you do not lose weight, you are probably sneaking in a few additional Calories from your diet or not effectively exercising. Do not whine or complain. There are only very few people on planet earth that will not shed their kilos in the face of Caloric deprivation. Fix it!

Survival Skills

Eating Out

The reality of life is that more and more of us eat out. We have little or no control over how the food we eat is prepared. So here are a few tips to get a better choice when eating out.

Eating from Hawker Stalls

Cheap and tasty, that is why hawker food is so popular. But many of the choices are high in fat, sodium and added sugars. So look around before you decide what to eat.

- If the hawker is about to cook your food request, ask for less oil and sauce to be added.

- At a pre-set meal cart, look at the choices and pick the items that seem to have less fat. Avoid deep-fried items and ask for less sauce or gravy.

- At the dessert and beverage stall, ask for less sugar or syrup to be added.

Portion Control

Ask for a smaller portion, but if you have no control over how much is placed on the plate, choose to eat less. If you are faced with a mound of food and know you do not want to waste the food, ask for the extra to be packed, take it home quickly, refrigerate, and then reheat it well before you eat it at another time.

Eating at Restaurants

From fast food to fine dining outlets, restaurants provide you with more choice. Read the menu and try to identify items that seem to need less fat and sugar. If in doubt, ask the counter staff or waiter. If you are unsure, be politely assertive and request for your food to be prepared with less fat and sugar.

Eating at Home

Shopping for Lower Calorie Foods
There are endless food choices on our supermarket shelves. With so much variety and so much food around us, it is hard not to buy too much.

- Before you get to the supermarket, make a list of the food you need and stick with it. This way, you will not bring the temptations home with you.

- Focus on getting the staples and necessities. Avoid loading the cart with treat foods.

- Do not shop when you are hungry. You will end up buying too much.

- At the supermarket, read food labels and compare food of the same category. Compare the values per 100 g rather than per serving as the serving size can vary. Pick the one that provides less Calories.

- Do not get carried away by products that flaunt tag lines such as being "low fat". Sometimes lower fat foods are not lower in Calories. As you are focused on weight loss, you need to check on the Calorie content.

Recipe Modification

Cooking for yourself will give you great control over what you choose to eat and how it is cooked. You do not have to be a great chef to prepare lower Calorie recipes. All you need to do is to learn four simple skills:

1 Replace

Study your favourite recipes to identify ingredients that are the highest sources of fat and added sugar. Think about suitable replacements. Test out the idea in a small portion. If it works, make the healthier recipe your regular choice.

Replacement Reckoner

- Full fat milk ➜ Low fat or skim milk
- Cheese ➜ Low fat cheese
- Fatty meat ➜ Lean meat (round, tenderloin or sirloin)
- Whole chicken or wings ➜ Skinless chicken breast or thighs
- Coconut milk ➜ Low fat coconut milk or low fat milk
- Sugar ➜ Fresh fruit juice or fresh or dried fruit

---

2 Reduce

Some recipes are classics and you may not be able to prepare them without a particular ingredient. Just use less.

Serve smaller portions. Stretch each dish to serve more people. This way everyone gets to taste the dish but no one has to overeat to finish the portion.

3 Lighten Up

Deep-frying or cooking with a lot of oil or cream can be replaced with healthier cooking styles. Steaming, boiling, roasting, baking, grilling or pan-frying using a nonstick pan are cooking methods that can be used instead.

4 Season for Flavour

Cooking with less fat and sugar will change the flavour of the original dish. So use a variety of herbs and spices, fresh and dried fruit as well as vegetables to create new combinations of flavours, aromas and textures to make up. Be creative.

Hit a Plateau? Gear Up! Do Not Give Up.

Losing weight is thrilling! This success is all you need to inspire you. After the thrilling ride down the weight loss spiral, sometimes you may hit a period when you find your weight is not moving down even though you seem to be eating and exercising as per your weight loss plan. Called the "plateau" in weight loss jargon, this is dangerous territory. Many well-intentioned dieters give up at this juncture. Here is what you can try to get over this hump:

Check Your Diet

Are you eating right? Check both your portions and the quality of your food choices? Perchance you picked up something that seemed innocuously low Calorie but in reality it is a Caloric minefield. Think nuts and seeds and such.

Check Your Exercise Plan

Now that you are lighter, your regular programme will burn less Calories. So, step up the intensity and the duration.

Keep Going

Here's where you need all the help you can get to keep you from turning your back on your weight loss plan. If the weight lever is not dipping left, focus away from the number and look for other motivating factors. Think about how much fitter you feel, how much better you look and such.

Breakfast

Will skipping breakfast help you cut down your Calorie intake? It seems logical, but nutrition experts report that this well-intentioned effort does not deliver the results hoped for. Here's why:

- Skipping breakfast leads to hunger and hunger drives the 'dieter' to eat more at lunch.

- When you are hungry, you tend to be less selective about food choices. You may indulge in any food you can find without considering the Calorie content.

So, if you are trying to shed weight, start the day right. Eat breakfast! Everyone has their preferred breakfast style:

- Are you a "quick and easy breakfast eater"? If so, your preference is for easy-to-prepare breakfasts such as cereal and milk, or a simple sandwich. The following pages will guide you in your selection of quick and easy breakfast options.

- Are you a "hearty breakfast eater"? If so, you enjoy a complete breakfast with more elaborate dishes and accompaniments to start the day. Read on for hearty breakfast options.

Whatever your preferred breakfast style may be, remember to get some wholesome nourishment before your rush into the day. And, believe it or not, you will be on track with your weight loss plan.

Eggs You Like It

Eggs are a cheap yet extremely nutritious food item. And they are very versatile too! Eggs can be prepared simply or used more creatively. For a 'dieter', it is an easy to prepare item that can be cooked in a variety of ways to add excitement to a lower Calorie meal plan. Eggs lend themselves to being the centrepiece at breakfast or a light snack. You can also include them as a light side item for a main meal. Plate up your eggy breakfast by picking one item from each column in the table below.

Egg	Bread	Side*
Sunny-side Up (page 38) 1 (53 g) 71 Cal	Wholemeal bread 1 slice (30 g) 73 Cal	Tomato, grilled 1 small (82 g) 15 Cal
Scrambled Egg (page 38) 1 (53 g) 71 Cal	Whitemeal bread 1 slice (29 g) 75 Cal	Mushrooms, grilled 1/4 cup (18 g) 4 Cal
Soft-boiled Egg (page 38) 1 (53 g) 71 Cal	High fibre white bread 1 slice (29 g) 69 Cal	Capsicum, grilled 1/4 cup (37 g) 10 Cal
Hard-boiled Egg (page 39) 1 (53 g) 71 Cal	Wholemeal bun 1 bun (35 g) 93 Cal	Reduced sugar baked beans 1/4 can (106 g) 88 Cal
Basic Omelette (page 39) 1 (53 g) 71 Cal	White bread 1 slice (29 g) 75 Cal	Cucumber 2 slices (14 g) 2 Cal

* Prepared without added fat

Nutrition Fact

Every teaspoon (5 ml) of oil added to cook eggs will add on 40 Calories. Most basic egg preparations do not need added fat or oil, so keep a tight reign on the amount of oil used for cooking.

Sunny-side Up

- Heat a nonstick pan. Crack an egg into the pan.
- Lower heat and cook until egg white turns white and egg yolk is cooked to a consistency of your preference.
- Remove from heat and serve hot.

Scrambled Egg

- Crack an egg into a small bowl. Season with salt and pepper to taste.
- Heat a nonstick pan. Pour prepared egg into the pan, lower heat and allow to cook until the egg begins to set.
- Stir gently to break up the egg curd. Continue cooking and stirring until the egg is scrambled.
- Remove from heat and serve hot.

Soft-boiled Egg

- Place egg in a small saucepan. Cover with cold water.
- Bring to boil over medium heat. Reduce heat and simmer.
- After 2–3 minutes, remove the egg with a slotted spoon and serve warm.

Hard-boiled Egg

- Place egg in a small saucepan. Cover with cold water.
- Bring to boil over medium heat.
- Remove from heat and leave to stand in the hot water for 4–17 minutes depending on whether you like your egg soft or hard.

Basic Omelette

- Crack an egg into a small bowl. Season with salt and pepper to taste.
- Heat a nonstick pan. Pour prepared egg into the pan.
- Swirl the pan to allow the egg to cover the base.
- Lower heat and allow the egg to cook for another 1–2 minutes until omelette is done. Serve warm.

Sandwich Mix & Match

Does your busy lifestyle dictate that all you can do for breakfast is to throw together a simple sandwich in less than 5 minutes? If so, here's a simple sandwich planner. Pick from a variety of breads, spreads and fillings to put together a breakfast that meets your allocated Calorie allowance. Go ahead, be creative!

Bread	Spread	Filling
Wholemeal bread 1 slice (30 g) 73 Cal	Butter 1 tsp (5 g) 34 Cal	Reduced fat cheese slices 1 slice (21 g) 41 Cal
	Soft margarine 1 tsp (5 g) 23 Cal	Turkey ham, extra lean 1 slice (20 g) 24 Cal
Soft grain bread 1 slice (29 g) 60 Cal		Tuna canned in water ⅓ can (52 g) 66 Cal
	Peanut butter, smooth 1 Tbsp (16 g) 94 Cal	Roasted chicken breast (fat-free) 1 slice (13 g) (11 Cal)
High fibre white bread 1 slice (29 g) 69 Cal	Fruit spread 1 Tbsp (20 g) 50 Cal	Hard-boiled egg 1 egg (53 g) 71 Cal
		Smoked salmon 1 slice (17 g) 20 Cal
White bread 1 slice (29 g) 75 Cal	Mayonnaise, light 1 Tbsp (15 g) 49 Cal	Canned sardines ⅙ can (70 g) 88 Cal
		Reduced sugar baked beans ¼ can (106 g) 88 Cal
	Mustard 1 tsp (5 g) 3 Cal	Lettuce 1 leaf (5 g) 1 Cal
Hot dog roll 1 roll (55 g) 156 Cal		Tomato 2 slices (54 g) 10 Cal
	Tomato chilli sauce 1 Tbsp (17 g) 18 Cal	Cucumber 2 slices (14 g) 2 Cal
Hamburger bun 1 bun (55g) 164 Cal	Kaya 1 Tbsp (9 g) 23 Cal	Alfalfa sprouts 1 Tbsp (3 g) 1 Cal

Today's Choice

- 2 slices wholemeal bread   **146 Cal**
- 1 Tbsp mayonnaise, light   **49 Cal**
- 1 slice turkey ham   **24 Cal**
- 1 lettuce leaf   **1 Cal**

▶ **220 Cal**

Tomorrow's Choice

- 2 slices wholemeal bread   **146 Cal**
- 1 tsp butter   **34 Cal**
- 1 Tbsp kaya   **23 Cal**

▶ **203 Cal**

Nutrition Tip

Make sure you have your basic breakfast items at hand to prepare a great sandwich early in the morning. Compare food labels to pick breakfast basics that are lower in Calories, then select those that deliver better nutritional value such as more fibre, healthier fats, vitamins and minerals.

Cereal Mix & Match

This is the snappiest breakfast you can put together. Shake the cereal into a bowl and top it with cold milk. Viola!! You are set to eat!

Ready to Eat Cereal of Choice	Milk of Choice	Topping
Whole grain cereal ½ cup (29 g) 106 Cal	Whole milk 1 cup (250 ml) 150 Cal	Raisins 1 Tbsp (10 g) 31 Cal
Cereal with banana chips, nuts ½ cup (30 g) (124 Cal)	Low fat milk (2% fat) 1 cup (250 ml) 122 Cal	Dried prunes 3 (25 g) 60 Cal
Cereal with dried blueberries ½ cup (22 g) (85 Cal)		Walnuts, sliced 1 Tbsp (8 g) 49 Cal
	Skim milk 1 cup (250 ml) 86 Cal	Almonds, sliced 1 Tbsp (6 g) 33 Cal
Oat cereal with honey ½ cup (20 g) (79 Cal)		Banana 1 small (100 g) 90 Cal
Cornflakes, plain 1 cup (28 g) (100 Cal)	Soy drink, unsweetened 1 cup (250 ml) 83 Cal	Fresh strawberries 3 small (21 g) 7 Cal

Nutrition Tip

Picking a lower Calorie ready to eat breakfast cereal is not easy. Sometimes the packaging and the names of the products suggest that the content of the box may be very healthy. But study the nutrition information panel and compare products. Pick the one that delivers less Calories per serving. Cereals that contain a lot of sugar, dried fruit and nuts tend to pack a lot more Calories in a smaller volume.

Cornflakes
1 cup (28 g) 100 Cal

Larger portion
(plain)

Today's Choice

- ½ cup whole grain cereal   **106 Cal**
- 1 cup skim milk   **86 Cal**
- 1 Tbsp raisins   **31 Cal**
- 1 Tbsp sliced walnuts   **49 Cal**

272 Cal

Tomorrow's Choice

- 1 cup cornflakes   **100 Cal**
- ½ cup low fat milk   **61 Cal**
- 1 small banana   **90 Cal**
- 1 Tbsp sliced almonds   **33 Cal**

284 Cal

Oat Cereal with Honey
⅔ cup (25 g) 100 Cal

Cereal with Dried Fruit and Nuts
⅖ cup (24 g) 100 Cal

Smaller portion
(with sugar & toppings)

Preparation time 5 minutes
Cooking time 10 minutes
Per serving 150 Cal

Oatmeal Porridge

This is a basic staple but it really is good for you! And it takes just a few minutes to cook. Low in fat and high in fibre, it is a healthy breakfast choice that can be a regular part of your lower Calorie strategy.

Makes 4 servings

Rolled oats 1½ cups (135 g)

Water 4 cups (1 litre)

Raisins 4 Tbsp (40 g)

Low fat milk ½ cup (125 ml)

- In a heavy-based pan, add oatmeal and water. Bring to boil, stirring regularly.

- Add raisins and continue to cook. Lower heat and cook for 2–3 minutes until done.

- Remove from heat and add milk. Stir and serve warm.

Nutrition Fact

Have a sweet tooth? Want to add a sweetener?

A tablespoonful of honey (21 g) will top up the energy content of your oatmeal porridge by 64 Cal.

A teaspoonful of brown sugar (3 g) will add 12 Cal.

Preparation time 10 minutes
Cooking time 10 minutes
Per serving 100 Cal

Mushroom & Cheese Toast

Crispy slices of toast with warm, soft toppings are irresistible. Try this nutrient-packed version to start your day off with tasty satisfaction that is hard to beat.

Makes 4 servings

Button mushrooms 16 (112 g), sliced finely

Wholemeal bread 4 slices (112 g each)

Low fat mozzarella cheese, grated 3 Tbsp (20 g)

Low fat cheddar cheese, grated 1 Tbsp (7 g)

- Place equal portions of sliced mushrooms on each slice of bread. Top with cheese.

- Grill at 180°C for 15 minutes until cheese melts and toasts turn golden brown.

- Serve immediately.

Nutrition Fact

Low fat cheeses are a great way to include calcium and protein in your diet without overloading on fat and Calories. If you are a cheese lover who cannot stomach the lower fat options, you may want to use smaller portions of the regular version.

	Mozzarella cheese, full fat (100 g)	Mozzarella cheese, low fat (100 g)	Cheddar cheese, full fat (100 g)	Cheddar cheese, low fat (100 g)
Energy (Cal)	300	254	403	173
Fat (g)	22	16	33	7

Preparation time 5 minutes
Cooking time 10 minutes
Per serving 155 Cal

Tuna Pita Pizza

Be creative to transform usual ingredients into something new. Here, the pita pocket is used as the base of a small pizza to prepare a healthier breakfast for a weight-conscious individual.

Makes 4 servings

Canola oil 1 Tbsp (15 ml)

Shallots 2, small (20 g), peeled and sliced fine

Green chilli ½ (5 g), sliced fine

Tuna canned in water ½ can (65 g), drained

Lemon juice 1 tsp

Ground white pepper to taste

Coriander leaves 2 sprigs, chopped

Chilli sauce 4 Tbsp (60 ml)

Wholemeal pita pockets 4 (120 g, each)

Tomato 1 (120 g), cut into 8 slices

Low fat mozarella cheese 4 Tbsp (27 g)

- Heat oil in a nonstick pan and stir-fry shallots and green chilli until fragrant.
- Add tuna and stir to flake well. Remove from heat.
- Season with lemon juice, pepper and coriander leaves.
- Spread 1 Tbsp chilli sauce over each pita bread.
- Spoon prepared tuna mixture equally among pita bases.
- Top each pita base with 1 Tbsp chilli sauce, 2 tomato slices and 1 Tbsp cheese.
- Grill in a preheated oven at 250°C for about 10 minutes until cheese melts and pizza base is crisp.
- Serve immediately.

Nutrition Fact

Many versions of canned tuna are available in the supermarket today. To make this pita pizza lower in fat and Calories, canned tuna in water is recommended. Did you know that water-packed tuna contains more omega-3 fats than oil-packed tuna?

	Water-packed tuna (100 g)	Oil-packed tuna (100 g)
EPA (g)	0.05	0.03
DHA (g)	0.22	0.10

Preparation time 10 minutes
Cooking time 20 minutes
Per serving 190 Cal

Fish Porridge

Rice porridge is a traditional breakfast choice across many parts of Asia. Most often, it is eaten plain with sauces, preserved vegetables, salted egg or fermented soy bean curd. Adding fish to this recipe not only enhances the flavour and nutritional value, but also makes it more satiating.

Makes 4 servings

Fish or vegetable stock 4 cups (1 litre)

Fish sauce 1 Tbsp (15 ml)

Sugar 1 tsp (3 g)

White fish fillet 200 g, sliced thinly

Rice 1 cup (150 g), washed and drained

Water 1 cup (250 ml)

Ginger 1 thumb-size knob (20 g), peeled and sliced thinly

Ground black pepper to taste

Spring onion 1 (10 g), sliced finely

- Bring stock to boil. Add fish sauce and sugar. Stir well.

- Add sliced fish and cook for about 1 minute, until fish slices are translucent. Remove fish from stock and set aside.

- Add rice, water and ginger to remaining stock and continue to cook for another 20 minutes until rice is well cooked and soft. Season with pepper.

- Portion into 4 bowls and serve hot, topped with fish and spring onion.

Nutrition Fact

For some, meals and snacks must have a certain volume to create a sense of satisfaction. Porridges, salads and soups go a long way if you need bulk at each meal. Protein in the meal also enhances the power to satiate so that you are not looking for a snack soon after.

Preparation time 5 minutes
Cooking time 10 minutes
Per serving 190 Cal

Japanese Cold Noodles

Japanese foods are the rave all over Southeast Asia, especially among the young and women. Here is a favourite that you can add to your breakfast options.

Makes 4 servings

Water 4 cups (1 litre)

Green tea soba 200 g

Cucumber 1, medium (360 g), peeled, cored and grated finely

Japanese soy sauce 2 Tbsp (30 ml)

Sesame oil 1 tsp (5 ml)

Seaweed 1 sheet (2 g), finely sliced

- Bring water to boil in a heavy-based pan.

- Add soba and cook until just done. The noodles should be cooked but firm. Drain well. Cool soba in a bowl of cold water and drain again. Chill until ready to serve.

- To serve, mix soba with grated cucumber.

- Portion soba into 4 bowls and drizzle with soy sauce and sesame oil.

- Garnish with seaweed. Serve immediately.

Nutrition Fact

Soba noodles are usually brown in colour and made from buckwheat flour. The green tea version has a pleasant green tone. Soba noodles deliver more protein for the same volume than rice noodles.

	Cooked soba noodles (100 g)	Cooked rice noodles (100 g)
Energy (Cal)	99	109
Protein (g)	5	1

Preparation time 10 minutes
Cooking time 15 minutes
Per serving 165 Cal

Fat-free Chapatti

If you are game for a relaxing bread-making session in your kitchen, start with chapatti. It is almost failure-proof. Chapatti served with lentils (page 56) is a staple in many Indian homes. Once you get the knack of preparing these two items, you will appreciate the natural wholesome goodness of this vegetarian option.

Makes 4 servings

Wholemeal flour 2 cups (220 g)

Salt ½ tsp (2 g)

Hot water ¾ cup (180 ml)

- In a large bowl, mix together flour, salt and water. Knead for about 10 minutes until dough is firm yet, soft and pliable. You may need to adjust the amount of water added depending on the flour type.

- Leave dough in the bowl and cover bowl with a wet cloth. Let dough stand for 30 minutes.

- Divide dough into 8 equal portions. Roll each portion into a ball.

- Sprinkle some flour on a clean work surface. Use a rolling pin to roll each ball of dough out into a circle.

- Heat a griddle. Place a chapatti on the griddle and allow to cook. Chapatti will puff up and then deflate. It is done when brown spots start appearing all over chapatti.

- Repeat to cook all chapatti. Serve hot with Lentil & Vegetables (page 56).

Nutrition Fact

You always knew wholemeal flour was better than the refined version and here is why. It delivers more protein, fibre and iron.

	Wheat flour, white (100 g)	Wheat flour, wholemeal (100 g)
Energy (Cal)	364	339
Protein (g)	10	14
Fibre (g)	3	12
Iron (mg)	1	4

Preparation time 10 minutes
Cooking time 20 minutes
Per serving 105 Cal

Lentil & Vegetables

An age-old accompaniment for chapatti, lentils provide protein of good value especially for avid vegetarians.

Makes 4 servings

Water 1 cup (250 ml)

Orange lentils ½ cup (100 g), washed and drained

Ground turmeric ¼ tsp

Onion ½, small (25 g), peeled and chopped

Ginger, ground into a paste 1 tsp (5 g)

Garlic 2 cloves (6 g), peeled and chopped

Green chilli 1 (10 g), sliced

Choko (chayote) ¼ (160 g), skinned and cut into cubes

Tomato 1, medium (100 g), cut into wedges

Lemon juice ½ Tbsp (7.5 ml)

Salt to taste

Coriander leaves 1 sprig

• In a heavy-based pan, place water, lentils, turmeric, onion, ginger, garlic and green chilli. Boil until lentils are soft.

• Add choko cubes and cook until tender.

• Add tomato. Season with lemon juice and salt.

• Remove from heat. Garnish with coriander leaves and serve hot.

Cooking Tip

Add tomato to the pan only towards the end of cooking. Old wives' tales suggest that the acid in tomatoes will prevent the lentil from cooking.

Nutrition Fact

Lentils are a good source of fibre, so it keeps you fuller for a longer time. They are also a good source of protein and are low in fat.

	Lentils, raw (100 g)	Chicken breast, uncooked (100 g)
Total fat (g)	1	16
Protein (g)	26	15
Fibre (g)	31	0

Preparation time 15 minutes
Cooking time 10 minutes
Per serving 160 Cal

Egg Omelette Wrap

A simple yet complete dish, this omelette can be eaten as a side dish
for lunch or dinner, or as a main dish for breakfast or snack.

Makes 4 servings

Chicken breast 1, skinned and sliced
  into thin strips

Canola oil 1 Tbsp (15 ml)

Garlic 2 cloves (6 g), peeled and
  minced finely

Shallots 2 (20 g), peeled and sliced
  finely

French beans 50 g, topped and tailed,
  sliced thinly

Carrot ⅓ medium (50 g), peeled and
  sliced into matchsticks

Cabbage ⅛ small head (100 g),
  sliced thinly

Salt to taste

Ground white pepper to taste

Eggs 2, beaten gently

Marinade

Teriyaki sauce 1 Tbsp (15 ml)

Corn flour 2 tsp (4 g)

Salt to taste

Ground white pepper to taste

- Marinate chicken with teriyaki sauce, corn flour, salt and pepper for 15 minutes.

- Heat half the oil in a nonstick pan. Stir-fry garlic and shallots until golden brown and fragrant. Add marinated chicken and cook until done.

- Add French beans, carrot and cabbage and cook until tender, stirring all the time.

- Season with salt and pepper. Remove from pan and set aside.

- Reheat nonstick pan and glaze with remaining oil. Add beaten eggs and swirl pan to form an omelette.

- Remove omelette to a plate and spoon prepared chicken and vegetable filling onto omelette. Fold omelette over into a semi-circle or fold into a parcel. Slice and serve with bread or rice.

Nutrition Fact

Egg is an inexpensive protein and has little effect
on your cholesterol when eaten in moderation.
In fact, it is the consumption of saturated fat that
has the greatest effect on your blood cholesterol.
If you are still concerned about cholesterol, you
can use two egg whites in place of one whole
egg or purchase lower cholesterol eggs.

Lunch

It is a fact of life. Sometimes you are just too busy to cook up an elaborate meal. At other times, you are eating alone. Often, you just want to tuck into a simple, light meal.

You may want to step out to pick up a lower Calorie lunch meal or put in a little extra effort and cook up a delicious lunch. Either way, the table below provides guidance to help you keep to your Calorie target.

For your convenience, we have grouped local hawker foods into three Caloric options. Pick a choice from the Calorie list that fits your plan.

We have also included some homemade dishes that will take less than 30 minutes to put together. Care has been taken to keep the fat content low and to moderate the portions.

One-dish meals fit nicely into lower Calorie meal plans. Try them for lunch and dinner. Not only will they help you save Calories, they will add many valuable nutrients to support your health.

Eating Out—Lower Calorie Options

Noodles in soup are going to be your lifeline if you do eat out. Not only are they larger in volume, they pack less Calories. The more fat a dish has, the smaller the portion you can consume. Try to start your lunch with a glass of water and end it with a slice of fruit. This strategy will help you feel full and also ensure nutritional completeness to your mid-day meal. A standard hawker portion of fruit may provide between 60 and 120 Calories.

Less than 300 Calories	301–400 Calories	400–500 Calories
Prawn noodle soup (574 g) 294 Calories	Prawn dumpling noodle soup (574 g) 399 Calories	Wonton with spinach noodles, dry (367 g) 480 Calories
Wonton noodle soup (545 g) 290 Calories	Sliced fish *beehoon* soup (686 g) 350 Calories	
Fishball *tunghoon* soup (527 g) 218 Calories	Chicken and mushroom noodle soup (653 g) 346 Calories	Chicken and mushroom noodles, dry (397 g) 441 Calories
Seafood *beehoon* soup (654 g) 297 Calories	Minced pork and mushroom noodle soup (597 g) 383 Calories	Wonton noodles, dry (330 g) 411 Calories

Preparation time 10 minutes
Cooking time 20 minutes
Per serving 400 Cal

Glutinous Rice

What seems to be a complicated dish is actually a simple recipe once you get organised.

Makes 4 servings

Chicken breast ½ (100 g), skinned and cut into cubes

Glutinous rice ¾ cup (140 g), washed and drained

Dried mushrooms 4 (14 g), soaked to soften, stalks removed and sliced thinly

Dried prawns 20 g, washed and drained

Light soy sauce 2 Tbsp (30 ml)

Fat-free chicken stock (page 88) 4 Tbsp (60 ml)

Peanuts 20 g, roasted

Marinade

Sesame oil 1 Tbsp (15 ml)

Light soy sauce 1 tsp (5 ml)

Ground white pepper a dash

- Marinate chicken cubes with sesame oil, soy sauce and pepper for 15 minutes.

- In a heatproof glass casserole dish, add rice, marinated chicken, mushrooms, dried prawns, soy sauce and stock.

- Steam for 20–25 minutes until rice is cooked.

- Garnish as desired and serve.

Cooking Tip

To know when the dish is ready, check the grain to ensure it is well done. Different grains may need a little more or less water. If the dish seems dry, increase stock as needed.

Nutrition Fact

This dish purchased from supermarkets and hawker stalls has a whopping 16 g (approx 3 tsp) fat per portion (147 g). This fat comes largely from the Chinese sausage, lard and fatty pork and this is mostly of the artery-clogging saturated type. This recipe contains only 6 g fat per portion (160 g), largely from the peanuts which provide mostly heart healthy monounsaturated fat. What's more, peanut is naturally free of cholesterol.

Preparation time 10 minutes
Cooking time 20 minutes
Per serving 290 Cal

Macaroni & Chicken Soup

*Keeping the protein choice lean and staying away from the fried toppings
makes this eternal staple a dieter's preferred dish.*

Makes 4 servings

Water 4 cups (1 litre)

Macaroni 2 cups (200 g)

Fat-free chicken stock (page 88)
6 cups (1.5 litres)

Chye sim ½ bundle (200 g), cut into
short lengths

Carrot ½ (120 g), peeled and cut
into strips

Chicken breast 1 (200 g), skinned

Salt to taste

Ground white pepper to taste

Sesame oil 1 tsp (5 ml)

- Boil water in a pot. Add macaroni and
  cook for 8 minutes until just done. Drain
  and place in a colander. Rinse with cool
  water and drain.

- Boil chicken stock in a pot. Blanch chye
  sim and carrot separately. Drain and set
  aside.

- Add chicken to stock and cook for
  8–10 minutes until just done. Drain, cool
  and slice thinly.

- Season soup with salt and pepper.

- Portion macaroni into 4 serving bowls.
  Top with chicken, chye sim and carrot.
  Pour over prepared chicken stock. Drizzle
  with sesame oil and garnish as desired.
  Serve immediately.

Cooking Tip

Cooked macaroni and other pastas swell when
they are in contact with water. So while you
can prepare ahead of time, do not leave pasta
soaking in soup or it will lose its 'bite'.

Nutrition Fact

Macaroni is a lower Calorie option
compared to popular instant noodles.

	Fried Instant Noodles (100 g)	Non-fried Instant Noodles (100 g)	Macaroni (100 g)
Energy (Cal)	457	332	371
Fat (g)	20	0	1.5

Preparation time 20 minutes
Cooking time 20 minutes
Per serving 490 Cal

Curry Noodles

Cooking concepts from the east and far east are combined to turn out this popular dish. Usually doused with coconut milk, the Caloric load of every serving tops the charts. This lower Calorie version retains the spices but holds back on the fat laden ingredients to present a lighter yet tasty version of the original preparation.

Makes 4 servings

Water 4 cups (1 litre)

Yellow noodles 400 g (14⅓ oz), washed and drained

Prawns 8, medium (130 g), cleaned

Firm tofu 1 block (200 g), cubes

Bean sprouts 100 g, topped and tailed, washed

Chye sim ⅓ bundle (150 g), washed and cut into short lengths

Curry gravy

Canola oil 2 Tbsp (30 ml)

Ginger 2 tsp (10 g), minced

Garlic 2 tsp (10 g), minced

Onion 1 (80 g), peeled minced

Curry powder 2 Tbsp

Water 4 Tbsp (60 ml)

Tomato 100 g, washed and minced

Salt to taste

Water 2 cups (500 ml)

Low fat evaporated milk ⅘ cup (200 ml)

Low fat coconut milk 2 Tbsp

Nutrition Fact

Coconut milk is a concentrated source of fat and so is chock-full of calories. But, it lends an amazing mouthfeel and flavour to curry dishes. In this lower fat version, coconut milk is replaced in large part with low fat evaporated milk. A regular bowl of curry noodles (532 g) from a hawker stall has about 809 Cal and 52 g fat. This recipe (500 g) brings you just 490 Cal and 14 g fat.

- Boil water in a pot. Blanch noodles, prawns, firm tofu, bean sprouts and chye sim separately. Drain and set aside.

- Heat oil in a nonstick pan. Add ginger and garlic and fry until fragrant. Add onion and fry until golden brown.

- In a bowl, mix curry powder with water. Add paste to onion mixture and cook until fragrant. Add tomato and season with salt. Continue to cook until oil separates from spice mixture.

- Add water and bring to boil. Lower heat and add evaporated milk and coconut milk. Remove from heat and stir well.

- To assemble dish, portion out noodles, prawn and vegetables into 4 serving bowls. Pour over curry sauce and serve.

Cooking Tip

When preparing curries with low fat milk, add the milk only at the last stage. Boiling the curry sauce may cause the milk to split as it comes into contact with the acidic ingredients such as tomato and this will not make the curry pleasant to look at. Add just a dash of coconut milk as a seasoning before you remove the pot from heat to capture the aroma of this natural flavouring. A lower fat coconut milk is available to help you lower the Calorie content of coconut-containing recipes.

Preparation time 15 minutes
Cooking time 15 minutes
Per serving 330 Cal

Char Kway Teow

A favourite indulgence in Southeast Asian countries such as Singapore and Malaysia, the evolution of this dish is steeped in Chinese cuisine but unique versions of this dish have become part of the local cuisine culture. The original recipes feature flat rice noodles served with a variety of seafood items, lathered with fat and dark soy sauce. This healthier version strips off the lard and tones down the sauces to uncover and present the natural flavours of fresh ingredients. Truly different from the original but still very delicious and attractive.

Makes 4 servings

Canola oil 3 Tbsp (45 ml)

Garlic 3 cloves (9 g), peeled and minced finely

Shallots 3 medium (30 g), peeled and sliced finely

Prawns 15, medium (250 g), peeled

Bean sprouts 150 g, topped and tailed, washed

Chye sim ⅓ bundle (150 g), cut into short lengths

Flat rice noodles 400 g, rinsed and drained

Eggs 2 (100 g), lightly beaten

Light soy sauce 1 Tbsp (15 ml)

Dark soy sauce a dash, just for colour

Salt to taste

Ground white pepper to taste

- Heat a nonstick wok. Grease the base with a little oil using paper towels.

- Add garlic and shallots and stir-fry lightly. Add prawns and cook until pink and tender. Remove from heat and set aside.

- Add remaining oil to wok and reheat wok. Add bean sprouts and stir-fry for 1–2 minutes. Remove and set aside. Repeat to cook chye sim.

- Add noodles and stir-fry for 2 minutes. Return vegetables to wok and mix well. Using a wok spatula, create a space in the centre of wok by moving the noodles and vegetables to the side. Add egg and cook until set. Scramble egg and mix well with noodles and vegetables. Toss in prawns.

- Season with soy sauces, salt and pepper.

- Dish out and serve hot garnished as desired.

Nutrition Fact

A plate of *char kway teow* (384 g) from the hawker stall has about 740 Cal and 38 g fat, with most of the fat being the heart unfriendly saturated type. This light version is lower in fat, especially saturated fat; and is full of vegetables.

Preparation time 20 minutes
Cooking time 20 minutes
Per serving 320 Cal

Seafood Tunghoon

Made from mung bean flour, glass vermicelli (tunghoon) is a favourite noodle in many east Asian countries. Usually cooked with flavourful stocks or sauces, the naturally mild noodle picks up these natural taste enhancers with ease.

Makes 4 servings

Prawns 6, large (240 g), peeled

Squid 110 g, cleaned and cut into bite-size pieces

Glass vermicelli (tunghoon) 200 g

Canola oil 1½ Tbsp (23 ml)

French beans 100 g, topped and tailed, sliced thinly

Carrot ¾ (100 g), peeled and sliced into matchsticks

Shallot 1, medium (10 g), peeled and sliced thinly

Garlic 3 cloves (9 g), peeled and minced finely

Fat-free chicken stock (page 88) ½ cup (125 ml))

Sugar 1 tsp (4 g)

Light soy sauce ½ tsp (3 ml)

Salt to taste

Ground white pepper to taste

Marinade

Light soy sauce 1 tsp (5 ml)

Sesame oil ½ tsp (3 ml)

Ground white pepper a pinch

- Marinate prawns and squid separately with light soy sauce, sesame oil and pepper.

- Soak vermicelli in water for 15 minutes to soften. Drain and set aside.

- Heat oil in a nonstick wok. Add prawns and stir-fry until just done. Remove from heat and set aside. Repeat to cook squid.

- Add French beans and carrot and stir-fry for 2–3 minutes. Remove from heat and set aside.

- In the same wok, stir-fry shallots and garlic until golden brown and fragrant.

- Add vermicelli and cook, stirring all the time. Add stock and allow noodle to cook until soft.

- Add prepared vegetables, prawn and squid. Season with sugar, soy sauce, salt and pepper.

- Cook for another 2 minutes. Remove from heat and serve hot, garnished as desired.

Nutrition Fact

Carbohydrates are perceived as fattening foods. But carbs per se—rice, noodles, bread—are not fattening. However, if it is cooked with lots of fat and the portion eaten is large, then the Calories peak. The way to keep the carbs in your diet is to hold the oil and eat a reasonable portion.

Preparation time 20 minutes
Cooking time 25 minutes
Per serving 525 Cal

Nasi Lemak

This Southeast Asian favourite features rice cooked in thick coconut milk as the main feature, making it high in fat and Calories. By using a lower fat coconut milk and reducing the amount of coconut milk, you can make this lower Calorie version a more regular feature in your meal plan.

Makes 4 servings

Rice 2 cups (300 g), washed and drained

Low fat coconut milk ¾ cup (180 ml)

Water 1 cup (250 ml)

Pandan leaves 2, knotted

Salt 1 tsp (4 g)

Egg 1 (50 g)

Peanuts 100 g

Dried anchovies (*ikan bilis*) 100 g

Bird's eye chillies 2, sliced thinly

Cucumber ½ (150 g), sliced

Tomato 1 (160 g), sliced

Sambal *belacan* to taste

- Place rice, coconut milk, water, pandan leaves and salt in a rice cooker. Cook until done.

- Place egg in a saucepan with enough cold water to cover completely. Bring to boil over high heat. Once water is at a rolling boil, reduce heat to a low medium boil and cook an additional 15 minutes for a hard-boiled egg. Remove from heat and place eggs in ice cold water. Peel and slice into 8 wedges. Set aside.

- In a microwaveable dish, mix together peanuts, dried anchovies and chilli. Microwave on High for 5 minutes, stopping twice to stir mixture. Remove and allow to cool.

- Serve rice with sliced egg, toasted dried anchovies and peanuts, cucumber and tomato. Serve with sambal if desired.

Nutrition Fact

Microwaving or toasting the dried anchovies gives you the crunchiness without adding fat and Calories. A few slices of raw cucumber and tomato adds a fair amount of fibre to this one-dish meal.

Preparation time 10 minutes
Cooking time 20 minutes
Per serving 290 Cal

Vegetable Pulao

Inspired by the Indian original, this healthier version includes generous portions of vegetables.

Makes 4 servings

Canola oil 2 Tbsp (30 ml)

Onion 1, medium (100 g), peeled and sliced finely

Garlic 1 tsp (5 g), minced finely

Green chilli 1 (10 g), sliced finely

Cinnamon stick 1

Cloves 2

Cardamom pods 2

Basmati rice 1 cup (180 g), washed and drained

Carrot ½ (100 g), peeled and cut into small cubes

Peas ½ cup (100 g)

Button mushrooms 8 (100 g), cut into small pieces

Canned kidney beans ¼ cup (60 g), drained

Salt to taste

Ground white pepper to taste

Water 1½ cups (375 ml)

- In a nonstick wok, heat oil and stir-fry onion until golden brown and fragrant. Add garlic and chilli and continue to cook for another minute, stirring all the time. Add spices and fry for another minute.

- Add rice and stir-fry until grains are dry and separate. Add carrot, peas, mushrooms and beans and stir-fry for 1–2 minutes. Season with salt and pepper.

- Transfer rice to a rice cooker. Add water and cook until done.

- Serve hot garnished as desired.

Nutrition Fact

Basmati rice is a low Glycemic Index (GI) food. When you eat basmati rice, it gets digested slowly and is converted to glucose gradually, therefore making you feel fuller for longer. This may help with weight control.

	Basmati rice (150 g)	Jasmine rice (150 g)
Glycemic Index (GI)	58	89
Glycemic Load (GL)	22	37

Preparation time 15 minutes
Cooking time 30 minutes
Per serving 460 Cal

Chicken Rice

Tender chicken, served with fragrant rice and spicy chilli-garlic sauce, delights the eye and the palate. Loaded with fat, and, rather substantial in portion, regular chicken rice is a 'no-no' on a lower Calorie meal plan, but with a few replacement tricks in place, you can try this healthy alternative without relish!

Makes 4 servings

Chicken breasts 2, whole (400 g)

Fat-free chicken stock (page 88)
  4 cups (2 litres)

Canola oil 2 Tbsp (30 ml)

Garlic 1 tsp (5 g), minced finely

Long-grain white rice 1½ cups (290 g),
  washed and drained

Salt 1 tsp (4 g)

Cucumber ½ (150 g), sliced

Tomato 1 (160 g), sliced

Sauce

Red chillies 3

Salt 1 tsp (5 ml)

Ginger 2 tsp (10 g), minced finely

Shallot 1 (10 g)

Garlic 2 tsp (10 g), minced finely

Sugar 1 tsp (4 g)

Vinegar ½ tsp (3 g)

Sesame oil ½ tsp (3 ml)

Lime juice 1 tsp (5 ml)

Marinade

Salt ¼ tsp

Ginger ½ tsp (3 g), minced finely

Canola oil ½ tsp (3 ml)

Light soy sauce ½ Tbsp (8 ml)

Sesame oil 1 tsp (5 ml)

- Marinate chicken breasts with salt, ginger paste, oil, soy sauce and sesame oil. Cover and leave refrigerated for at least 30 minutes.

- Bring stock or water to boil in a large heavy-based pot. Lower in marinated chicken and simmer for 6–8 minutes. Remove from heat and immerse in a pot of cold water for 10 minutes to chill quickly. Drain and set aside.

- Heat a nonstick wok. Add oil and stir-fry garlic and rice until grains are dry and separate. Season with salt. Transfer rice to a rice cooker and cover with 2½ cups (625 ml) chicken stock and cook till done.

- Blend sauce ingredients in a food processor into a smooth paste.

- Serve prepared rice with chicken and sauce, tomatoes and cucumber slices. Garnish as desired.

Cooking Tip

Cooking lean poultry is challenging as overcooking makes the meat even tougher and drier. To preserve the tenderness and moistness of the chicken, plunge the cooked meat in cold water to stop the cooking process.

Nutrition Fact

Chicken breast is the leanest cut of the bird. Remove the skin and the fat content of the lean cut drops by a further 71 per cent.

Preparation time 25 minutes
Cooking time 15 minutes
Per serving 340 Cal

Oriental Fried Rice

This traditional one-dish meal may have been created to use up leftovers or to be a time saver, but its staying power over the centuries attests to its popularity even today. This healthier version scales down on fat, sodium and preserved foods, plays up the wholegrains and vegetables, and is served with toasted nuts for a modern twist.

Makes 4 servings

Long-grain white rice ½ cup (100 g), washed and drained

Brown rice ½ cup (100 g), washed and drained

Fat-free chicken stock (page 88) 4 cups (1 litre)

Canola oil 3 Tbsp (45 ml)

Eggs 2 (100 g), lightly beaten

Onion ½ (35 g), peeled and finely minced

Garlic ½ tsp (3 g), minced finely

Green, red and yellow capsicums ½ each, (240 g altogether), cut into small cubes

Fresh shiitake mushrooms 2 (30 g), cut into small cubes

Salt to taste

Ground black pepper to taste

Lean ham 90 g, thinly sliced

- Using a rice cooker, cook white and brown rice separately with chicken stock. Set aside to cool.

- Heat 1 Tbsp oil in a frying pan and add beaten eggs. Swirl pan to form a thin omelette. When omelette is set, remove from pan. Slice thinly when cool.

- Heat remaining oil in a heavy-based wok and stir-fry onion and garlic until fragrant. Add capsicums and mushrooms and stir-fry for a few minutes until capsicums are almost done.

- Add both types of cooked rice and continue to fry over high heat. Season with salt and pepper.

- Top with ham and serve immediately, garnished as desired.

Cooking Tip

Cooking brown rice requires more water and more time than white rice. To work smart, cook and chill a portion of brown rice in your refrigerator ahead of time. Warm up the required portion and add it to the recipe.

Nutrition Fact

A hawker serving of fried rice (428 g) delivers a whopping 907 Cal on a plate with 33 g of fat. This smaller and healthier version (180 g) delivers 567 Cal less per serve!

Capsicum or bell pepper is packed with vitamin C. It contains 6 to 14 times the amount of vitamin C as tomatoes by weight.

	Green capsicum	Red capsicum	Yellow capsicum	Tomato
Vitamin C (mg) per 100 g	80	127	183	13

Preparation time 15 minutes
Cooking time 25 minutes
Per serving 500 Cal

Nasi Biryani

This recipe has travelled from the Middle East to several parts of Asia. A delectable flavoured rice dish cooked with meat, it has picked up local nuances wherever it has travelled. The original recipe is high in fat, but this healthier version cuts back on the fat and Calories while retaining the flavour to earn a place in your lower Calorie diet.

Makes 4 servings

Chicken

Chicken drumsticks 4 (550 g)

Ginger ½ Tbsp (3 g), minced finely

Garlic ½ Tbsp (4 g), minced finely

Non-fat yoghurt ½ cup (123 g)

Ground turmeric ½ tsp (1 g)

Ground coriander ½ Tbsp (4 g)

Chilli powder 1 tsp (3 g)

Ground black pepper to taste

Salt to tase

Tomatoes 2 (230 g), cut into quarters

Green chilli 1 (10 g), split

Large onions 2 (200 g), cut into quarters and bruised slightly by pounding

Mint leaves a handful, chopped

Coriander leaves a handful, chopped

Rice

Canola oil 1 Tbsp (15 ml)

Cinnamon stick 1

Cardamom pods 2

Cloves 3

Basmati rice 1½ cups (280 g), washed and drained

Salt to taste

Water 1½ cups (375 ml)

- Marinate chicken with ginger, garlic, yoghurt, ground turmeric and coriander, chilli powder, pepper and salt. Cover and refrigerate for 30 minutes.

- Place marinated chicken, tomatoes, green chilli, onions, mint and coriander leaves in a heavy-based pot and cook over medium heat until chicken is three-quarters cooked.

- Start preparing rice. In another pan, heat oil and fry cinnamon, cardamoms and cloves for about 30 seconds to enhance flavour. Add drained rice and stir-fry for 3–5 minutes until grains are dry and separate. Add salt to taste. Transfer prepared rice into a rice cooker, cover with measured water and cook till grains are just done.

- Transfer rice to a deep serving dish and layer with prepared chicken. Serve hot garnished with cashew nuts and coriander leaves, if desired. Serve with a fresh salad or raita (Indian salad with yoghurt).

Cooking Tip

Marinating chicken with yoghurt helps to tenderise the lean meat.

Nutrition Fact

Nasi biryani served with spicy chicken (488 g) usually contains nearly 35 g fat and 880 Cal. This lower fat and healthier recipe was created just for *nasi biryani* lovers! It fills you up and supplies only 500 Cal and 13 g fat.

Dinner

Even as you track down on the weighing scale, you still need food to fulfill your basic Calorie and nutrient needs.

Focus on getting the four main foods groups—grains, proteins, fruit and vegetables—together in the best meal of your day. This combination is a pleasure both to the eye and the palate.

Worried about putting in more Calories at the end of the day? Ever heard that you should have the lightest meal before you sleep? The evidence that holds water today is that no matter at what time you eat, you just need to cut back on your total Calorie intake and push up your activity level to achieve the Calorie deficit. Timing of meals is not the cause of weight gain nor the barrier to weight loss.

Pick your meal combination from the soups, salads, main entrees, sides and staples to build a delicious meal that is within your Calorie allowance for dinner.

Soups & Salads

Soups

Soups are naturally high in water content. Prepared with care,
they can be flavourful and very low in fat. Use soups at the beginning
of your meal to take the edge off hunger and bulk up on refreshing fluid.

Asian soups are usually clear. Stocks are painstakingly prepared by
simmering flavourful ingredients for hours at a time. This also helps release
fats form the meat into the stock. To save substantial Calories, prepare the
stock ahead of time, chill and remove the layer of fat that rises to the top.
Reheat the stock and add vegetables and lean cuts of meat to boost the
nutrient level of your soup.

Western soups that are thick and creamy are often a Caloric challenge.
Modify the recipe to use less fat and replace cream to achieve a lighter
version.

Salads

Salad ingredients—vegetables and fruit—are naturally lower in Calories than
ingredients used to make up main meals. They also deliver more fibre, vitamins
and minerals per Calorie.

Eaten fresh with light dressings, vegetables and fruit are bulky and take up
space in your stomach, displacing other Calorie-dense foods. So a smart dieting
strategy would be to eat a salad before your meal.

Watch the dressings. Many popular dressings are very high in fat and Calories.
Use them sparingly to flavour your salads.

Preparation time 12 minutes
Cooking time 1 hour
Per serving 20 Cal (without chicken)

Chicken & Melon Soup

Makes 4 servings

Winter melon 400 g, skinned
and cubed

Red dates 8

Fat-free Chicken Stock

Water 8 cups (2 litres)

Chicken ½ (600 g), skin removed

Garlic 1 medium clove, peeled and
pounded roughly

Salt to taste

Ground white pepper to taste

- Prepare chicken stock. Boil water in a
  pot. Add chicken and garlic and return to
  the boil for 2 hours.

- Strain stock. Discard chicken and bones.
  Season with salt and pepper.

- Leave stock to cool, then refrigerate and
  skim off layer of fat. This stock can be
  used in other recipes requiring fat-free
  chicken stock.

- Bring stock to boil. Add winter melon and
  red dates. Garnish as desired. Serve hot.

Nutrition Fact

Have you come across the popular soup
diets? Soup diets such as cabbage and onion
soups have been around for ages and many
claim that they help you shed quite a few
kilos just within a week. There is no magic
in the broth. It just provides a low Calorie
filler that takes up all the space in your
tummy, displacing everything else. Carried
out over long periods, these diets will throw
up nutritional deficiencies.

Preparation time 10 minutes
Cooking time 3 hours
Per serving 75 Cal (without ribs)

Pork Rib & Lotus Root Soup

Another traditional favourite, this wholesome soup takes pride of place in many Chinese homes. By selecting leaner cuts of ribs and defatting the soup stock, even the strictest of dieters can indulge in a fair share of this meal opener.

Makes 4 servings

Water 10 cups (2.5 litres)

Pork ribs 500 g

Lotus root 250 g

Peanuts 60 g

Red dates 10

Scallops 20 g

- Boil 2 cups (500 ml) water in a heavy-based pot. Add pork ribs and cook for 5 minutes. Drain.

- In another pot, bring remaining 8 cups (2 litres) water to boil. Add pork ribs, lotus root, peanuts, red dates and scallops. Bring to a rolling boil, then lower heat and simmer for 3 hours.

- To further lower the fat content, cool stock and refrigerate overnight. Skim off layer of fat and reheat.

- Serve hot with rice and vegetables. Garnish as desired.

Nutrition Fact

Don't throw out the lotus root when serving this soup. Ten slices of lotus root (81 g) has about 4 g dietary fibre. Fibre has satiating power and supports bowel regularity.

Preparation time 10 minutes
Cooking time 20 minutes
Per serving 90 Cal

Carrot Soup

Thick vegetable soups can up a substantial snack or part of a main meal. Naturally rich in vitamins, minerals and fibre, vegetables are fat-free and filling.

Makes 4 servings

Fat-free chicken stock (page 88) or water 4 cups (1 litre)

Carrots 4, medium (600 g), peeled and cut into cubes

Onion 1, medium (100 g), peeled and cut into cubes

Garlic 1 clove (3 g), peeled and lightly smashed

Salt to taste

Ground white pepper to taste

Butter 1 Tbsp

- Boil stock or water in a pot. Add carrots, onion and garlic and cook until carrots are soft. Season with salt and pepper. Remove from heat and cool well.

- Blend cooled stock together with cooked ingredients in a food processor until smooth.

- Reheat just before serving and flavour with butter. Garnish as desired.

Cooking Tip

To maximise the natural nutrients in carrot, reserve the water in which the carrot is boiled to make up part of the soup base. For more flavour, add a portion of other vegetables such as celery and potatoes.

Nutrition Fact

Orange-coloured vegetables and fruit are excellent sources of vitamin A. Carrots offer twice as much vitamin A (16,000 IU) than pumpkin (7384 IU).

Butter lends an aroma and mouthfeel that cannot be replaced in some recipes. But can you afford the butter? 1 Tbsp butter delivers around 11.5 g fat and 100 Cal. If your weight is not dropping fast enough, skip the butter.

Salad Mix & Match

There simply are no rules when it comes to creating a salad. For basics, start with a single vegetable and drizzle it with a lower Calorie salad dressing. As you get more adventurous, combine vegetables, experiment with some sweet fruit and add lean meat to create your own salad creations. Here is a Salad Planner to get you started.

Vegetable / Fruit Starter	Protein Toppings	Garnishes	Dressings
Fresh Vegetables	Hard-boiled egg 1 (53 g) 71 Cal	Sesame seeds 1 Tbsp (8 g) 50 Cal	Lemon juice 1 Tbsp (15 g) 4 Cal
Lettuce, 1 leaf (5 g) 1 Cal			
Tomato, 2 slices (54 g) 10 Cal			Vinegar 1 Tbsp (15 g) 3 Cal
Cucumber, 2 slices (14 g) (2 Cal)	Canned tuna in water, ⅓ can (52 g) 66 Cal		Yoghurt, non-fat 1 Tbsp (14 g) 7 Cal
Carrot, ½ cup (64 g) 26 Cal		Pine nuts 1 Tbsp (8 g) 57 Cal	
Capsicum, ½ cup (74 g) 20 Cal			Yoghurt, low fat 1 Tbsp (15 g) 10 Cal
Cabbage, ½ cup (45 g) 11 Cal	Roasted chicken breast, skin removed 1 slice (13 g) 11 Cal		
Celery, ½ cup (51 g) 7 Cal			Light soy sauce 1 Tbsp (17 g) 13 Cal
Cooked Vegetables		Almonds 1 Tbsp (6 g) 33 Cal	
Sweet corn, ⅓ cup (55 g) 44 Cal			Plum sauce 1 Tbsp (19 g) 35 Cal
Sweet peas, ½ cup (72 g) 55 Cal	Smoked salmon 1 slice (17 g) 20 Cal		
Broccoli, ½ cup (78 g) 27 Cal			Fish sauce 1 Tbsp (18 g) 6 Cal
Carrot, ½ cup (78 g) 27 Cal			
Potato, ½ cup (78 g) 68 Cal	Soy bean curd, firm ¼ block (27 g) 28 Cal	Walnuts 1 Tbsp (8 g) 49 Cal	Satay sauce 1 Tbsp (15g) 39 Cal
Fresh Fruit			
Watermelon, ½ cup (76 g) 23 Cal			Mayonnaise, light 1 Tbsp (15 g) 49 Cal
Apple, with skin, ½ cup (55 g) 29 Cal	Garbanzo beans, canned 1 Tbsp (15 g) 17 Cal		Thousand Island, light 1 Tbsp (17 g) 23 Cal
Pineapple, ½ cup (83 g) 37 Cal		Cashew nuts 1 Tbsp (9 g) 50 Cal	
Orange segments, ½ cup (90 g) 42 Cal	Kidney beans, canned 1 Tbsp (16 g) 13 Cal		French Dressing, light 1 Tbsp (16 g) 32 Cal
Mango, ½ cup (83 g) 54 Cal			Caesar Dressing, light 1 Tbsp (15 g) 17 Cal
Dried Fruit			
Raisins, 1 Tbsp (10 g) 31 Cal	Low fat cottage cheese 1 Tbsp (14 g) 10 Cal	Peanuts 1 Tbsp (9 g) 53 Cal	Italian Dressing, light 1 Tbsp (14 g) 28 Cal

Dressings Compared

	Mayonnaise	Thousand Island	French Dressing	Caesar Dressing	Italian Dressing
Regular (1 Tbsp)	100 Cal	60 Cal	73 Cal	77 Cal	43 Cal
Light (1 Tbsp)	49 Cal	23 Cal	32 Cal	17 Cal	28 Cal

Preparation time 20 minutes
Per serving 70 Cal (without prawns); 105 Cal (with prawns)

Citrus Pomelo

Asian salads are characterised by plain or tangy vegetables garnished with spicy or tangy sauces that pick up their uniqueness from spices and herbs rather than fat.

Makes 4 servings

Bean sprouts 70 g, topped and tailed

Prawns 200 g, peeled

Pomelo 200 g, peeled and segmented, pith removed

Oranges 300 g, peeled and segmented, pith removed

Green capsicum 75 g, cored and sliced

Cucumber 100 g, sliced

Honey cherry tomatoes 4, halved

Onion 1, small (90 g), peeled and sliced finely

Spring onion 1, chopped finely

Lime juice 3 tsp (15 ml)

Mint leaves 2–3 sprigs, optional

- Boil a pot of water and blanch bean sprouts lightly. Drain.

- Boil a fresh pot of water and blanch prawns until they turn pink and are cooked. Drain.

- Mix together pomelo and orange segments with capsicum, cucumber and bean sprouts. Toss in prawns, honey tomatoes, sliced onion and spring onion. Refrigerate to chill.

- Just before serving drizzle over lime juice and sprinkle with mint leaves. Stir well and serve.

Nutrition Fact

Adding prawn into the salad peps up its nutritional value. Prawns provide protein, selenium, zinc as well as omega-3 fats. As they do contain cholesterol, portion control is the key to enjoying prawns without guilt.

Preparation time 10 minutes
Per serving 55 Cal

Watermelon Salad

Makes 4 servings

Watermelon 600 g, cut into cubes, seeded

Salted fish 1 small piece (15 g), washed, toasted and pounded finely

Spring onions 2, chopped finely

Lime juice 3 tsp (15 ml)

White sesame seeds 1 Tbsp, toasted

- In a large bowl, combine watermelon cubes with salted fish and spring onions. Refrigerate to chill.

- Just before serving, add lime juice and toss watermelon cubes.

- Drizzle with toasted sesame seeds and serve.

Cooking Tip

When lime juice is added to the watermelon, it leaches out the water, so add it just before serving. Prepare just enough as this salad does not keep well.

Nutrition Fact

This Asian-style salad takes very little time to prepare. As watermelon is mostly water, it is generally low in Calories—a cup of watermelon (152 g) provides only 46 Cal! Watermelon is a good source of the antioxidant lycopene. Add just a sprinkling of sesame seeds to enhance the flavour of this salad as sesame seeds provide a lot of fat if eaten in large quantities.

Main Dishes

Main Dishes

Protein-rich dishes are usually the feature of a main meal. Whether you ascribe to a meatless diet or are a regular meat eater, remember that protein provides nourishment that helps you repair and maintain your body.

While we do need good quality proteins, we do not need too much of it either, so keep your protein portion moderate. A simple rule of thumb is to keep the portion of cooked meat, fish or poultry to the size of your palm.

Focus on getting lean or low fat ingredients to start your dish. Review your favourite recipes and strip off all the ingredients that add more fat. Then spice up and flavour these dishes with herbs and spices. Choose a cooking method that preserves the flavour but does not load up on more added fat, such as steaming, grilling, baking and pan-frying.

Preparation time 5 minutes
Cooking time 5 minutes
Per serving 200 Cal

Easy Sardines

Makes 4 servings

Canola oil ½ Tbsp (7.5 ml)

Onions 2, large (200 g), peeled and sliced finely

Ginger 0.5-cm knob (15 g), peeled and minced finely

Green or red chilli 1 (10 g)

Sardines in tomato sauce 1 can (325 g)

- Heat oil in a nonstick pan. Stir-fry onions, ginger and chilli until fragrant.

- Add sardines and cook until dry.

- Garnish as desired. Serve hot with rice or bread.

Nutrition Fact

When you are in a rush, canned sardines are a convenient way to add protein and calcium to your meals. Reduced fat and lower sodium canned sardines are now available.

Preparation time 20 minutes
Cooking time 12 minutes
Per serving 120 Cal

Baked Whole Trevally

Spice mixtures added to this baked fish help bring out the best of the flavour without any dependence on fat. Vary the fish types and the spice mixtures to discover your favourite baked fish recipe.

Makes 4 servings

Yellowband trevally 1 (300 g), cleaned

Sambal belacan 2 tsp (10 g)

Minced garlic ½ tsp (3 g)

Minced ginger ½ tsp (3 g)

Lemongrass 1 stalk (30 g), ends trimmed, tough outer leaves removed and sliced finely

Salt to taste

Ground white pepper to taste

Onion ½ (50 g), medium, peeled and sliced thinly into rings

Coriander leaves or spring onion as desired

- Make 2–3 diagonal cuts on each side of fish.

- In a food processor, blend together *sambal belacan*, minced garlic and ginger, lemongrass, salt and pepper into a paste.

- Rub paste on fish, cover and leave for 10–15 minutes.

- Preheat oven to 180°C.

- Place fish on a sheet of aluminium foil large enough to wrap fish and top with onion rings. Wrap fish into a parcel with foil.

- Place parcel on a baking tray and bake for 12 minutes.

- Unwrap parcel and check that fish is cooked by inserting a fork into the flesh. The fork should go through easily.

- Garnish with coriander or spring onion and serve.

Nutrition Fact

Have you heard that chilli may increase fat loss by speeding up the metabolism rate? Do spices such as chilli really offer hope of weight loss for overweight people? Some recent studies suggest that capsaicin found in chillies may increase the oxidation of fat. This may be good news for those who love spicy food, but we need more research to be done on this before we are able to make the recommendation related to weight loss.

Preparation time 8 minutes
Cooking time 20 minutes
Per serving 170 Cal

Steamed Sea Bass

A mild and moist fish presented with pungent Asian spices—chilli and ginger— and encased with traditional soy sauce and rice wine, makes the ultimate health dish. Served often within homes and also at Chinese restaurants, this fish recipe is well appreciated for its presentation and taste.

Makes 4 servings

Sea bass 1 (580 g), cleaned

Spring onions 20 g, chopped

Red chilli 1 (10 g), slit, seeded and sliced

Young ginger a small knob (15 g), peeled and sliced thinly

Chinese parsley 20 g

Light soy sauce 2 Tbsp (30 ml)

Sesame oil ½ Tbsp (7.5 ml)

Rice wine 1 Tbsp (15 ml)

Ground white pepper a dash

- Make 2–3 diagonal cuts on each side of fish and place fish on a steaming plate.

- Top with spring onions, chilli, ginger and parsley. Drizzle with soy sauce, sesame oil, wine and pepper.

- Place steaming plate in a steamer and steam for 18–20 minutes until fish is soft and flesh flakes with ease when tested with a fork.

- Remove from heat and serve with rice and vegetables.

Cooking Tip

Are you sensitive to the fishy aroma of steamed fish? Lessen the smell by rubbing a little lemon juice onto the flesh and skin before washing the fish. Steam with extra ginger and add a few wedges of tomato to disguise the fishy note.

Nutrition Fact

Fish is a good source of protein and is lower in saturated fat and cholesterol than red meats or poultry. Steaming helps conserve flavour and uses very little oil.

Preparation time 10 minutes
Cooking time 10 minutes
Per serving 180 Cal

Spicy Sesame Salmon

Makes 4 servings

Salmon fillet 300 g

Minced garlic ½ tsp (3 g)

Minced ginger ½ tsp (3 g)

Salt to taste

Ground white pepper to taste

White sesame seeds 2 Tbsp (20 g), toasted

Dried red chilli 1 (2 g), washed, seeded and chopped very finely

Coriander leaves 20 g, chopped very finely

Spring onion 1 (15 g), chopped very finely

Canola oil 1 tsp (5 ml)

Thai chilli sauce 2 Tbsp (30 ml), optional

- Marinate salmon fillet with garlic and ginger, salt and pepper for 10 minutes.

- Combine sesame seeds, dried chilli, coriander leaves and spring onion. Coat salmon on skinned side with this sesame seed mixture.

- Heat a nonstick frying pan and coat lightly with oil. When pan is very hot, place salmon with coated side face down on pan.

- Let salmon brown, then turn it over and cook other side until skin is golden brown and crisp, taking care not to overcook fish. If preferred, fish can remain translucent and orange (like a medium rare steak).

- Serve warm with a drizzle of Thai chilli sauce.

Cooking Tip

Never overcook salmon. A well finished salmon fillet retains the beautiful pink hue and moist tenderness on the inside. Crispy, golden brown salmon skin can be achieved by using high heat.

Nutrition Fact

Salmon is a great source of high-quality protein and omega-3 fats. Omega-3 fats may support heart health and deliver potential benefits for skin and joint health too.

Preparation time 10 minutes
Cooking time 15 minutes
Per serving 200 Cal

Salmon & Vegetable Parcel

Makes 4 servings

Salmon fillet 400 g, divided into
   4 portions

Sake 2 Tbsp (30 ml)

Japanese soy sauce (*shoyu*) 1 Tbsp
   (15 ml)

Sugar snap peas 8

Fresh shiitake mushrooms 40 g,
   stalks removed, cleaned with a
   moist cloth

Fresh button mushrooms 30 g, stalks
   removed, cleaned with a moist cloth

Carrot ¼ (50 g), peeled and cut into
   matchsticks

Spring onions 2 or about 8 stalks

Salt to taste

- Marinate salmon with sake and soy
  sauce for 15 minutes. Drain and reserve
  marinade.

- Preheat oven to 190°C.

- Place each salmon slice on a sheet of
  aluminium foil large enough to wrap
  salmon.

- Boil a pot of water and blanch sugar
  snap peas. Remove and drain.

- Arrange mushrooms, carrot and sugar
  snap peas on fish, then place a spring
  onion diagonally across the vegetables.

- Drizzle with marinade and wrap up with
  foil to make four parcels.

- Place parcels on a baking tray and bake
  for 15–20 minutes.

- Unwrap and serve with rice or noodles to
  complete the meal.

Cooking Tip

Baking in aluminium foil helps to keep the fish
moist and tender as the cooking is achieved
by steam generated from heating the fish and
vegetables.

Nutrition Fact

Salmon is considered a "fatty fish",
but the fat in salmon, which is
predominantly omega-3 fats, is heart
healthy. When used in the right portion,
slamon can be part of your healthful
weight loss strategy.

Preparation time 10 minutes
Cooking time 15 minutes
Per serving 150 Cal

Pan-fried Cod Fillet with Glazed Vegetables

Cod infused with Asian flavours and served on a bed of colourful fruit and vegetables makes a delicious yet low Calorie main dish.

Makes 4 servings

Cod fish fillet 400 g, divided into 4 portions

Light soy sauce 1 tsp (5 ml)

Salt to taste

Ground white pepper to taste

Canola oil 1 Tbsp (15 ml)

French beans 100 g, cut into short lengths

Carrot 1 (100 g), cut into short lengths

Onion 1 (100 g), peeled and sliced into rings

Mandarin orange segments or mango strips 40 g

- Marinate fish with soy sauce, salt and pepper. Cover and leave for 20 minutes.

- Heat ½ Tbsp oil in a nonstick frying pan and pan-fry fish until golden brown on the outside and tender on the inside.

- Boil a pot of water and blanch beans and carrot. Drain and set aside.

- In a heavy-based wok, heat remaining oil and fry onion until golden brown and fragrant. Add beans and carrot and cook until tender. Season with salt and remove from heat.

- Plate vegetables on a serving dish, top with pan-fried cod and garnish with orange segments or mango strips. Serve immediately.

Cooking Tip

If fresh Mandarin oranges are not in season, use those canned in juice or light syrup. Drain the syrup before use to cut back on Calories and added sugar.

Nutrition Fact

Despite the tenderness of cod fish, it is a very low fat fish, with less than 1 g of fat for every 100 g portion.

	Cod fish (100 g)	Salmon, farmed (100 g)
Energy (Cal)	82	208
Fat (g)	1	13

Preparation time 15 minutes
Cooking time 15 minutes
Per serving 150 Cal

Tangy Assam Prawns

Naturally low in fat, prawns are a low Calorie seafood choice. Accompanied with a tangy sweet Asian sauce, this main dish is best served with a bowl of steaming hot rice and a vegetable side dish.

Makes 4 servings

Tamarind pulp 40 g

Water 4 Tbsp (60 ml)

Prawns 300 g, shelled and deveined

Plum sauce 1 Tbsp (15 ml)

Dark soy sauce ½ tsp (3 ml)

Sugar ½ tsp (3 g)

Salt to taste

Canola oil 1 Tbsp (15 ml)

Ginger 10 g, peeled and sliced thinly

Spring onion 1 (30 g), cut into short lengths

- Place tamarind pulp in a small bowl and add water. Mix well, then strain to remove seeds and fibre. Set extracted liquid aside.

- In a separate bowl, marinate prawns with plum sauce, dark soy sauce, sugar and salt. After 15 minutes, remove prawns from marinade. Set marinade aside.

- Heat ¾ Tbsp oil in a nonstick wok over high heat. Stir-fry prawns until just pink and tender. Remove from heat and set aside.

- Heat remaining ¼ Tbsp oil in wok and stir-fry ginger until golden brown. Add marinade and tamarind water and cook until slightly thick.

- Turn off heat and add prawns and spring onion. Stir well and serve immediately.

Cooking Tip

Like all other seafood, overcooking makes prawn meat tough. To avoid this, use high heat to quickly stir-fry the prawns so that they retain their moistness and tenderness. You will know prawns are cooked when they turn pink.

Nutrition Fact

Weight for weight, prawns contain more cholesterol than most fishes, so keep the delicious treat for special occasions and when you do enjoy them, keep the portion small.

Preparation time 10 minutes
Cooking time 20 minutes
Per serving 100 Cal

Chicken Breast with Spicy Mango Salad

A dash of tang and spice lends an irresistible and refreshing touch to the healthy choice of chicken breast.

Makes 4 servings

Chicken breast 1 (200 g), skin, fat and bones removed

Minced ginger ¼ tsp (1.25 g)

Minced garlic ¼ tsp (1.25 g)

Corn flour ½ tsp (1.5 g)

Salt to taste

Ground white pepper to taste

Plum sauce 1 Tbsp (15 ml)

Thai chilli sauce 1 Tbsp (15 ml)

Salad

Cold water 1 cup (250 ml)

Vinegar 1 Tbsp (15 ml)

Salt ½ tsp (3 g)

Onion 1 (100 g), peeled and sliced thinly

Mango ½ (100 g), skinned, stoned and sliced thinly

Bird's eye chilli 1, minced finely

- Cut chicken breast into 4 pieces. Place chicken in a small bowl and marinate with ginger and garlic, corn flour, salt and pepper for 30 minutes.

- Wrap each marinated chicken portion in aluminium foil and bake at 180°C for 20 minutes.

- Remove chicken from foil and reserve any juices.

- Prepare a sauce by mixing together the chicken juices with plum sauce and Thai chilli sauce.

- Prepare salad. In a small bowl, add cold water, vinegar and salt. Add sliced onion and mix well. Drain and set aside. Mix onion, mango and chilli together.

- Serve chicken with prepared salad and drizzle with sauce.

Cooking Tip

Preparing skinned chicken breast is a challenge as the lean meat tends to toughen when cooked. Marinating the lean meat with a little corn flour helps to hold in the moisture. Wrapping the marinated chicken in foil before cooking also helps to retain its tenderness.

Nutrition Fact

Chicken breast is the leanest cut of the chicken. Removing the skin and all visible fat is a great technique to lower fat and energy content.

Preparation time 20 minutes
Cooking time 15 minutes
Per serving 140 Cal

Mini Chicken Patties

These versatile meat and vegetable patties make healthier burger fillings and are delectable served with rice and vegetables for a balanced meal.

Makes 4 servings

Chicken breast 1 (200 g), skin and fat removed, minced

Carrot ¼ (20 g), peeled and minced finely

French beans 3 (30 g), minced finely

Coriander leaves 1 Tbsp (1 g), minced finely

Green chilli ½ (10 g), minced finely

Minced garlic ½ tsp (3 g)

Minced ginger ½ tsp (3 g)

Corn flour 2 tsp (6 g)

Salt to taste

Ground black pepper to taste

Egg 1 (50 g), lightly beaten

Breadcrumbs ⅓ cup (30 g)

Canola oil 1 Tbsp (15 ml)

Plum sauce 2 tsp (10 ml)

- Mix together minced chicken, carrot, French beans, coriander leaves, chilli, minced garlic and ginger, corn flour, salt and pepper. Divide into 4 portions and shape each portion into a pattie.

- Dip each pattie in beaten egg and coat with breadcrumbs.

- Heat a frying pan and coat lightly with oil. Pan-fry patties one at a time until golden brown on both sides.

- Serve warm with a little plum sauce.

Cooking Tip

Pan-fry using a lightly oiled nonstick pan to achieve the golden brown colour and crunchy texture that patties are famed for. Do not overcook patties to maintain the moist succulence.

Nutrition Fact

Removing skin and visible fat from chicken reduces the fat and Calorie content substantially.

	Chicken with skin (100 g)	Chicken without skin (100 g)
Energy (Cal)	237	188
Fat (g)	14	7

Calorie and fat savings: 21 per cent Calories and 45 per cent fat

Preparation time 15 minutes
Cooking time 10 minutes
Per serving 160 Cal

Spicy Chicken with Cashew Nuts

Another classic turned into a healthier version. If you do not compare, this recipe turns out a pleasant dish to accompany your main meals.

Makes 4 servings

Chicken breasts 1½, skin and fat removed, cut into cubes

Canola oil 1 Tbsp (15 ml)

Dried red chillies 20 g, soaked, then split and deseeded

Raw cashew nuts 20 g, toasted

Spring onion 1, cut into short lengths

Marinade

Light soy sauce 1 Tbsp (15 ml)

Sugar 1 tsp (5 g)

Minced garlic ½ tsp (3 g)

Sesame oil 1 tsp (5 ml)

Ground white pepper to taste

Salt to taste

Sauce

Light soy sauce 1 Tbsp (15 ml)

Corn flour 1 tsp (2 g)

Vinegar 1 tsp (5 ml)

Sugar ½ tsp (2 g)

- Marinate chicken with light soy sauce, sugar, garlic, sesame oil, pepper and salt for 15 minutes.

- Heat oil in a nonstick wok and stir-fry dried chillies until fragrant. Remove and set aside.

- Add chicken and cook until done.

- Add cashew nuts and ingredients for sauce. Stir well. Add spring onion and remove from heat.

- Serve with rice and a portion of greens for a balanced meal.

Nutrition Fact

Cashew nuts are loaded with protein, fibre, minerals such as iron, magnesium and selenium. Just 15 cashew nuts supply approximately 145 Calories. Keep each portion small and avoid the deep-fried and sugared versions.

Preparation time 8 minutes
Cooking time 45 minutes
Per serving 130 Cal

Roast Lean Pork

This Asian-inspired hearty roast will take the pride of place as the main dish at your dinner table.

Makes 4 servings

Lean pork loin 350 g
Minced garlic 1 tsp (5 g)
Minced ginger ¼ tsp (1.3 g)
Black bean paste ½ Tbsp (7.5 ml)
Sugar 1 tsp (4 g)
Light soy sauce 2 tsp (10 ml)
Five-spice powder ½ tsp (1 g)
Salt to taste
Ground white pepper as needed

• Use a fork to pierce pork several times. Marinate pork with all other ingredients. Cover and refrigerate for 1 hour.

• Preheat oven to 250°C.

• Place marinated pork loin on a baking tray and roast for 10 minutes.

• Lower heat to 120°C and continue to roast for another 20 minutes.

• Use a meat thermometer to check that the internal temperature of meat has reached 65°C.

• When done, place on a cutting board and cover with a sheet of aluminium foil and allow to rest for 15 minutes.

• Slice and serve with rice and vegetables.

Cooking Tip

Slow roasting the pork loin keeps the meat moist and tender.

Nutrition Fact

Select lean pork always. The leanest pork cuts are the round and loin. Lean loin cuts have 34 per cent less fat and 11 per cent less energy than cuts with fat.

Preparation time 30 minutes
Cooking time 10 minutes
Per serving 230 Cal

Sweet & Sour Pork

Fatty, fried and sweet—the original version of this classic Chinese recipe is definitely a no-no in a low Calorie meal plan. This healthier version delivers on the tangy richness, enhances the vegetable portion and cuts back on fat.

Makes 4 servings

Lean pork 420 g, cut into small cubes

Canola oil 1 Tbsp (15 ml)

Red capsicum ¼ (20 g), cored, seeded and sliced

Green capsicum ¼ (20 g), cored, seeded and sliced

Cucumber 90 g, cut into cubes

Ripe pineapple 90 g, cut into cubes

Marinade

Salt ½ tsp

Ground white pepper ½ tsp

Corn flour 2 Tbsp

Chinese cooking wine 1 Tbsp

Light soy sauce 1 Tbsp

Sauce

Fat-free chicken stock (page 88) 3 Tbsp (45 ml)

Tomato sauce 3 Tbsp (45 ml)

Light soy sauce 1 Tbsp (15 ml)

Corn flour 2 tsp (6 g)

Alternative sweetener 2 tsp

- Marinate pork with salt, pepper, corn flour, wine and light soy sauce. Cover and set aside for 15 minutes.

- Heat a nonstick wok and coat with a little oil. Pan-fry pork cubes until golden brown and crispy on the outside.

- Heat a clean wok and coat with a little oil. Stir-fry capsicums lightly, then add cucumber and pineapple. Toss in pork cubes. Stir well.

- Mix together ingredients for sauce in a bowl. Add to wok and cook until sauce is thickened. Serve immediately with rice or noodles.

Nutrition Fact

A portion of sweet and sour pork (300 g) from a typical hawker stall has approximately 34 g fat and 600 Cal. If you grill or pan-fry the pork instead of deep-frying, you will reduce the fat content to only 9 g and lower the energy content to 230 Cal.

Preparation time 15 minutes
Cooking time 30 minutes
Per serving 250 Cal

Beef Stew

Stews are renowned for their natural intensity and depth of flavour and aroma. Hardier vegetables such as potato and carrots absorb the meaty flavour and add contrasting textures to the dish. The simple one-pot cooking style is also fat-free and fuss-free. Serve stews up with rice, bread or potatoes to complete the meal.

Makes 4 servings

Lean beef 250 g, cut into cubes

Cinnamon stick 1, about 7.5-cm long, broken into 2–3 pieces

Cloves 2

Star anise 1

Water 4 Tbsp (60 ml)

Butter 1 Tbsp (15 ml)

Olive oil 1 Tbsp (15 ml)

Garlic 40 g, peeled and minced

Onion 1 (100 g), peeled and cut into wedges

Potatoes 2 (250 g), peeled and cut into cubes

Carrot 1 (120 g), peeled and cut into cubes

Celery stalk 1 (50 g), cut into cubes

Fresh button mushrooms 100 g

Light soy sauce 1 Tbsp

Dark soy sauce ½ Tbsp

Black peppercorns ½ Tbsp

Water 4 Tbsp (60 ml)

Corn flour 1 Tbsp

- Place beef, spices and water in a pressure cooker. Cover and cook for 15 minutes until beef is done. Drain meat, reserve stock.

- In a heavy-based pan, heat butter and olive oil. When butter is melted, add garlic and onion and stir-fry until fragrant and transparent but not brown.

- Add cooked beef, potatoes, carrot, celery and mushrooms and stir-fry for 5 minutes.

- Add stock, soy sauces and peppercorns and cook until vegetables are tender. Add corn flour slurry to thicken gravy.

- Remove from heat and serve hot with bread rolls or rice.

Cooking Tip

Cooking lean meat requires skill. Slow cooking at a lower temperature will render the lean meat softer. Add a slice or two of raw papaya to the pressure cooker before cooking the beef. The natural enzyme (papain) in papaya will help tenderise the meat even more.

Nutrition Fact

Round and sirloin are the leanest cuts of beef. Avoid using meat that is marbled with fat and remove any visible fat before cooking.

Did You Know?

There are many unfounded fears about red meat (beef, pork and lamb). Lean cuts of red meat are a good source of iron. Recent cancer prevention recommendations from the American Institute for Cancer Research state that a red meat portion of no more that 500 g per week is not a risk factor. So select a good cut, but keep the total portion small.

Serves 4
Preparation time: 10 minutes
Per serving 30 Cal

Japanese Cold Tofu

Tofu is a great source of protein and calcium and very moderate in natural fat content. Versatile in application, it can be served chilled or cooked.

Makes 4 servings

Silken tofu 1 block (240 g), chilled and cut into cubes

Tamari soy sauce 2 tsp (10 ml)

Sake 1 tsp (5 ml)

Sesame oil 1 tsp (5 ml)

Seaweed sheet 1 (3 g), sliced thinly

White sesame seeds 1 tsp (3 g), toasted

- Place tofu cubes on a serving plate.
- Mix together soy sauce, sake and sesame oil. Drizzle over tofu.
- Garnish with seaweed and sesame seeds. Serve chilled.

Nutrition Fact

Like meat, tofu is a good source of protein, but has a lower saturated fat content than meat. Tofu is also rich in calcium. In addition to supplying nutrients for your body to function properly, isoflavones found in tofu may also provide heart and bone health related benefits.

Preparation time 10 minutes
Cooking time 10 minutes
Per serving 240 Cal

Pan-fried Firm Tofu

Vegetables tend to have a lower Calorie density than other foods. They add variety and are a must-have in a well-balanced diet. Here, colourful and flavourful mushrooms and celery brighten up the plain and simple flavours of tofu.

Makes 4 servings

Canola oil 2 Tbsp (30 ml)

Firm tofu (*taukwa*) 2 blocks (450 g)

Garlic 2 cloves (6 g), peeled and minced finely

Hon shimeji (brown beech) mushrooms 130 g

King oyster (eryngii) mushrooms 100g

Celery ½ stalk (50 g), sliced

Oyster sauce 2 Tbsp (30 ml)

Light soy sauce 1 Tbsp (15 ml)

Corn flour 1 Tbsp

Water 4 Tbsp (60 ml)

- Heat a nonstick pan and coat lightly with a little oil.

- Place a block of firm tofu on the pan and pan-fry until golden brown on all sides. Do the same for the other block of firm tofu. Slice into cubes when cool.

- In the same nonstick pan, heat remaining oil and stir-fry garlic until golden brown.

- Add mushrooms and celery and stir-fry for 10 minutes until tender yet crunchy.

- Add firm tofu cubes and stir well.

- In a bowl, mix together sauces, corn flour and water. Add sauce to pan and continue to heat until sauce thickens slightly.

- Dish out and serve hot with rice and other main dishes.

Cooking Tip

Pan-frying can be an effective way of lending colour, texture and flavour to a dish. A lightly greased, well-heated pan ensures that fat absorption is minimised.

Nutrition Fact

Firm tofu is a good source of protein. If used to replace meat, it helps to lower the fat and cholesterol content of the meal. Steam, grill, pan-fry or braise firm tofu to include it in a lower Calorie diet. Avoid deep-frying to cut back on Calories.

Side Dishes

Side Dishes

Most Asian eating styles include several side dishes. These are usually a variety of cooked vegetables prepared with herbs and spices.

While vegetables are naturally low in Calories, preparing it with oil, especially large amounts of oil, really loads up the energy content of the dish. Some cuisines serve vegetables seasoned with fatty meat cuts to enhance the flavour.

Vegetables have an important place in the dieter's meal plan, so pick up some tips to seal in the nutrients and the flavours while reducing the dependence on fats and oils.

At home, steaming is your best choice. Alternatively, serve vegetables in a fat-free chicken stock. If you do stir-fry, bring out the nonstick pan and glaze the bottom with oil or a cooking spray. If you do want to use a little added oil, remember to measure it out carefully.

Eating out is regular part of many lifestyles. But before you order your vegetables, do the 'look test'—any vegetable coated in a layer of oil or deep-fried is likely not to be the lower calorie choice. If the veggies are smothered in coconut based gravies or deep-fried before being coated with sauce, stay away. If there really are no options, ask for the dish to be served without sauce or gravy.

Preparation time 30 minutes + 1 hour for soaking mushrooms
Cooking time 30 minutes
Per serving 60 Cal

Broccoli & Mushrooms in Sauce

The brilliant colours of this popular Chinese vegetable dish will enhance any main meal. Chock-full of nutrients, this low Calorie crowd pleaser also delivers intense flavours in every mouthful.

Makes 4 servings

Water 2 cups (500 ml)

Dried Chinese mushrooms 6 (20 g), soaked to soften, stems discarded

Broccoli 1 small head (100 g), separated into florets

Canola oil ½ Tbsp (7.5 ml)

Garlic 1 clove (3 g), peeled and minced

Sauce

Teriyaki sauce 1 tsp (5 ml)

Oyster sauce 1 tsp (5 ml)

Fat-free chicken stock (page 88) 1 tsp (5 ml)

Corn flour 2 tsp (6 g)

- Boil water in a pot. Add mushrooms and cook for about 30 minutes until soft and tender. Drain and set aside.

- Steam broccoli until tender. Remove from heat and set aside.

- Combine ingredients for sauce in a bowl.

- Heat oil in a wok and stir-fry garlic until fragrant. Add sauce and stir until slightly thickened.

- Add cooked broccoli and mushrooms. Stir well.

- Dish out and serve hot with rice and other main dishes.

Cooking Tip

Steaming broccoli helps retains most of the heat sensitive nutrients such as vitamin C and folate.

Nutrition Fact

Broccoli is a good source of fibre, vitamins A, C, E, folate and the mineral, potassium. A cruciferous vegetable, broccoli is a source of suphoraphanes, a natural phytochemical that may help the body ward off cancer. Shiitake mushrooms contain lentinan which may help support immune defenses of the body.

Nutrient Retention

	Steamed	Boiled with little water, covered	Boiled with excess water, covered and drained
Vitamin C (%)	85	80	75
Folate (%)	85	70	65

Preparation time 10 minutes
Cooking time 20 minutes
Per serving 80 Cal

Spinach with Eggs

This traditional Chinese recipe brings together a variety of eggs to enhance the flavour of the spinach, all in an extremely low calorie fashion. The cooking method is ever so simple that even a novice in the kitchen can prepare this with little fuss.

Makes 4 servings

Salted egg 1

Water 2 cups (500 ml)

Spinach 700 g, stems and roots discarded, washed and drained

Fat-free chicken stock (page 88) 1²/₃ cups (400 ml)

Salt to taste

Ground white pepper to taste

Century egg 1, peeled and cut into small pieces

- Boil a pot of water and lower in salted egg to cook for 15 minutes. Remove from heat, cool and shell. Cut into small pieces.

- In a clean pot, boil 2 cups water and blanch spinach leaves for about 1 minute. Drain and refresh in cool water. Drain and set aside.

- Bring chicken stock to boil and season with salt and pepper as needed.

- In a serving bowl, plate spinach and top with prepared salted and century eggs.

- Dish out boiling stock and serve immediately with rice and other main dishes.

Nutrition Fact

Although spinach contains iron, it also has oxalic acid which limits the absorption of iron. As spinach is packed with powerful antioxidants such as beta-carotene, lutein and zeaxanthin as well as vitamin K and folate, get the most out of this vegetable by having a piece of vitamin C-rich fruit with your meal to enhance the absorption of iron.

Preparation time 5 minutes
Cooking time 8 minutes
Per serving 90 Cal

Stir-fried Kailan

Green leafy vegetables are a must in a healthy diet. This simple and basic cooking method turns a variety of greens into presentable sides for any home table. So experiment with chye sim, xiao bai cai and other greens available in your market.

Makes 4 servings

Canola oil 1 Tbsp

Garlic 2 cloves (6 g) peeled and minced finely

Shallot 1 (20 g) peeled and sliced finely

Kailan 2 bundles (300 g), washed and cut into short lengths

Carrot ½, medium (125 g), peeled and cut into thin slices

Salt to taste

Ground white pepper to taste

- Heat a nonstick wok. With a spoon, lightly grease the sides of the wok.
- Add garlic and shallot. Stir-fry until golden brown and fragrant.
- Add vegetables and stir-fry for 1–2 minutes to allow vegetables to soften yet remain tender and crisp.
- Season with salt and pepper. Remove from heat and garnish as desired.
- Serve hot with rice and other main dishes.

Cooking Tip

You can replace kailan with chye sim, spinach or any green leafy vegetable. As you experiment, you will be able to control the heat and timing of cooking to turn out crisp and tasty vegetables to accompany your main meals. For variety, replace salt with light soy sauce to enjoy the distinct Chinese flavour.

Nutrition Fact

Dark green leafy vegetables such as kailan are good sources of disease-fighting phytochemical. In addition, they contain rich amounts of vitamin K, vitamin C and calcium.

Vegetables are fat-free, but adding fat or oil during cooking increases the Caloric content of vegetables tremendously. So as you experiment with various cooking styles to enjoy our daily dose of vegetables, keep a tight reign on added fat.

Preparation time 5 minutes
Cooking time 10–12 minutes
Per serving 25 Cal

Xiao Bai Cai in Broth

This dish presents green leafy vegetables with just enough broth to make it delicious, yet not too much to qualify the dish as a soup. It is an interesting way of transforming the humble vegetable to a side dish of esteem.

Makes 4 servings

Xiao bai cai 300 g, washed

Dried scallops 8, small (50 g)

Chinese wolfberries 1 tsp

Fat-free chicken stock (page 88)
  2 cups (500 ml)

- Place vegetables in a heatproof serving dish. Top with scallops and wolfberries.

- Pour stock over.

- Steam for 10–12 minutes to cook vegetables until tender.

- Serve hot with rice and other main dishes.

Cooking Tip

This easy-to-cook dish is packed with nutrients and is highly recommended to those who don't have much time to cook. Instead of stir-frying, a combination of steaming and boiling is used in this recipe. Be creative. Replace xiao bai cai with other green leafy or delicate vegetables of choice.

Nutrition Fact

Fat-free chicken stock is a must-have standby in a healthy kitchen. This basic ingredient usually makes its way as a base in soups, a flavour enhancer in main dishes and an alternative to adding more oil in stir-fried dishes.

Preparation time 15 minutes
Cooking time 10 minutes
Per serving 120 Cal

Stir-fried Long Beans with Squid

Adding a portion of squid to this simple stir-fry enhances its flavour and visual appeal. Try this technique with other vegetables to make them more attractive and nutritious.

Makes 4 servings

Canola oil 1 Tbsp (15 ml)

Garlic 2 cloves (6 g), peeled and minced finely

Shallots 2, medium (40 g), peeled and sliced thinly

Long beans 300 g, washed and cut into short lengths

Squid 100 g, cleaned and cut into bite-size pieces

Salt to taste

Ground white pepper to taste

- Heat oil in a nonstick pan. Add garlic and shallots and stir-fry until golden brown.

- Add long beans, cover and cook until tender.

- Add squid and cook until just done. Season with salt and pepper.

- Dish out and serve hot with rice and other main dishes.

Nutrition Fact

Here's the Calorie content for some common long bean dishes that we enjoy at hawker stalls.

	Long beans stir-fried with soy bean paste (100 g)	Long beans stir-fried with eggs (100 g)	Long beans stir-fried with sambal (100 g)
Energy (Cal)	77	80	100
Fat (g)	4	6	8
Protein (g)	4	4	4

Preparation time 10 minutes
Cooking time 10–15 minutes
Per serving 40 Cal

Steamed Pumpkin with Wolfberries

The pleasant sweetness of this fruity vegetable will make your meal interesting. Steamed to preserve nutrients and conserve on oil required, this simple recipe is a breeze for any one who wants to prep a meal in a hurry.

Makes 4 servings

Pumpkin 500 g, skin removed and cut into cubes

Chinese wolfberries 2 Tbsp, washed and drained

- Place pumpkin cubes in a heatproof dish. Sprinkle with wolfberries.
- Steam for 10–15 minutes until pumpkin is soft.
- Serve hot with rice and other main dishes.

Cooking Tip

This simple dish does not require any additional seasoning to enhance its flavour. Try it and see!

Nutrition Fact

Pumpkins and wolfberries contain an important antioxidant, beta-carotene. Beta carotene is converted to vitamin A in the body and has a role in eye health. Despite its intense natural sweetness, a whole cup of pumpkin provides just 50 Cal.

Preparation time 30 minutes
Cooking time 15 minutes
Per serving 90 Cal

Steamed Aubergines

Aubergines are widely available in Asia. They are often deep-fried or cooked with a lot of oil. Here, the intense flavours of lean pork and scallops add rich dimensions to the plain steamed aubergine.

Makes 4 servings

Lean pork 60 g, sliced thinly

Dried scallops 10 g

Water 4 Tbsp (60 ml)

Aubergines (eggplants/brinjals)
2 (220 g), slit through the centre

Garlic 4 cloves (10 g), peeled

Shallot 1, small (10 g), peeled

Canola oil 1 Tbsp

Spring onion 1, sliced

Marinade

Sesame oil 1 tsp

Light soy sauce 2 tsp

Dressing

Light soy sauce 2 tsp

Black vinegar 1 tsp

Sesame oil 1 tsp

- Marinate lean pork with sesame oil and soy sauce for 10 minutes.

- Soak scallops in 4 Tbsp water for 30 minutes. Shred finely.

- Place sliced aubergines on a heatproof plate. Top with marinated lean meat and scallops. Steam for 10–12 minutes until meat and aubergines are cooked.

- Heat a nonstick pan and add oil. Stir-fry garlic and shallot until fragrant.

- Garnish steamed aubergines and meat with fried garlic and shallot.

- Mix ingredients for dressing together and pour over prepared vegetables. Garnish with spring onion.

- Serve hot with rice and other main dishes.

Cooking Tip

While deep-fried aubergine dishes taste good and retain the vegetable's colour well, steaming is a close runner-up for flavour and colour retention. To prevent blackening of the cut edges of the raw aubergine or losing the intensity of the purple of the skin after steaming, prepare this dish just before serving.

Nutrition Fact

Aubergine is naturally low in fat but it absorbs more oil compared to other vegetables. Believe it or not, a small portion of fried aubergine with chilli (170 g) from the economic rice stall provides 15 g fat and 160 Cal.
This delicious steamed aubergine (85 g) gives you a wide range of nutrients but is low in fat and Calories.

Preparation time 30 minutes
Cooking time 15 minutes
Per serving 70 Cal

Stir-fried Ladies Fingers

A touch of spice and tanginess is added to this simple dish of ladies fingers. Traditional recipes require the spice paste to be basted and browned in excess oil to bring out the zest and coat the vegetable. This healthier version plays on the spices but tones down the oil to achieve a close match.

Makes 4 servings

Canola oil 1 Tbsp (15 ml)

Garlic 3 cloves (10 g), peeled and minced finely

Onion 20 g, peeled and sliced thinly

Sambal belacan 2 Tbsp (30 g)

Ladies fingers 400 g, topped and tailed, then slit through the centre

- Heat oil in a nonstick pan and stir-fry garlic and onion until golden brown.

- Add *sambal belacan* and stir-fry until fragrant.

- Add ladies fingers and cook for about 10 minutes until tender.

- Dish out and serve hot with rice and other main dishes.

Cooking Tip

Many Asian dishes require deep-frying or cooking in plenty of oil to keep the ladies fingers from exuding the mucin that some find rather gross. Wash ladies fingers before cutting, then cut into large pieces to reduce excess formation of mucin.

Nutrition Fact

A regular serving of this dish from a hawker stall would provide about 150 Cal for a standard serving of 120 g. This recipe delivers just 70 Cal for a similar 120 g portion. Ladies fingers are a great source of fibre. Just one serve provides 3 g fibre—quite a substantial amount when you need to only aim for 25–30 g fibre each day.

Preparation time 20 minutes
Cooking time 30 minutes
Per serving 205 Cal

Ngoh Hiang

Makes 4 servings

Prawns 100 g, peeled and minced finely

Lean pork 200 g, minced finely

Water chestnuts 4 (80 g) peeled and minced

Celery 40 g, minced

Carrot 40 g, minced

Parsley 20 g, minced

Spring onion 20 g, minced

Garlic 2 cloves (6 g), peeled and minced

Corn flour 2 Tbsp

Sesame oil 1 tsp (5 ml)

Five-spice powder ½ tsp

Egg 1 (50 g)

Salt to taste

Ground white pepper to taste

Dried bean curd skin 4 square sheets, about 20 x 20-cm, wiped with a clean, damp cloth

Canola oil 2 Tbsp

- In a bowl, mix together all ingredients except bean curd skin and oil.

- Place a bean curd sheet on a flat work surface with a corner pointing towards you. Spoon a quarter of meat mixture in a line on bean curd sheet, near the corner facing you. Fold left and right corners over meat mixture, then roll bean curd sheet up to make a neat roll. Seal with some water. Repeat to make another 3 rolls.

- Steam rolls for 20 minutes until meat and vegetables are cooked.

- Heat a nonstick pan and coat with a little oil. Pan-fry rolls until golden brown on the outside.

- Remove from heat, slice and serve.

Cooking Tip

As this dish requires some preparation, prepare the portions ahead of time in the weekends, then steam and store refrigerated without pan-frying. When ready to serve, steam to reheat the rolls, then pan-fry.

Nutrition Tip

A typical serving of *ngoh hiang* (434 g) from the hawker stall has 664 Cal. This smaller and healthier version (150 g) provides just 205 Cal per serving and is by far richer in vegetables and fibre than the original.

Snacks & Beverages

It is a fact that the less you eat, the larger will be the Caloric deficit you can create each day. So if you can avoid snacking, that's great for your diet! However, not many dieters can abstain from snacking. In fact, well planned snacks may prevent you from getting very hungry. When you are hungry, it is hard to be rational about food choices.

Healthy, lower Calorie snacks can be worked into your meal plan to help you enjoy a variety of foods, stay within your Calorie allowance and even, provide valuable nutrients to nourish you.

Use the following Snack Planner that lists 50, 100 and 150 Calorie snacks that are easily available in hawker centres, food courts and supermarkets. Pick a snack from any one of the lists and build it into your meal plan for the day to stay well within your Calorie allowance.

Snack Planner

We snack for many reasons but if you can stay away from snacking, that's great! If you must snack, then snack smart! Pick small portions of food or beverages to fit into your overall Calorie Allowance. And you can still have your snack and shed the weight.

Less than 50 Calories	50–100 Calories	101–150 Calories
Local Desserts		
Mango pudding 1 small cup (100 g) 47 Cal	*Guilinggao* (Herbal jelly) 1 serving (237 g) 70 Cal White fungus, lotus seed dessert ½ serving (167 g) 80 Cal	Bean curd ⅓ serving (206 g) 105 Cal *Cheng teng* ½ serving (248 g) 109 Cal Green bean soup ½ serving (215 g) 118 Cal Sweet potato soup ½ serving (246 g) 150 Cal
Beverages		
Diet cola 1 glass (250 ml) 0 Cal Fresh tomato juice 1 glass (279 ml) 42 Cal Fresh watermelon juice ½ glass (217 ml) 48 Cal	Barley water 1 glass (237 ml) 55 Cal Skim milk 1 cup (250 ml) 86 Cal Honeydew milkshake 1 glass (350 ml) 92 Cal Fresh carrot juice 1 glass (294 ml) 91 Cal Soy drink, unsweetened 1 cup (250 ml) 83 Cal	Soy drink, sweetened 1 cup (250 ml) 138 Cal Low fat milk (2% fat) 1 cup (250 ml) 122 Cal Whole milk 1 cup (250 ml) 150 Cal
Tidbits		
Popcorn, fat-free 1 cup (8 g) 16 Cal Rice cracker, baked 1 serving (7.5 g) 36 Cal	Baked red bean bun 1 whole (32 g) 102 Cal Chicken *pau* ½ serving (45 g) 107 Cal Wheat crackers, plain 1 serving (20 g) 82 Cal Cornflakes, plain 1 cup (28 g) 100 Cal Steamed *soon kway* 1 serving (72 g) 88 Cal *Chwee kway* 1 serving (57 g) 56 Cal *Putu mayam* 1 piece (50 g) 98 Cal	*Chee cheong fun* with sauce 1 serving (100 g) 133 Cal Vegetable *pau* 1 whole (77 g) 150 Cal *Ang koo kuih*, green bean 1 serving (70 g) 141 Cal Pandan chiffon cake 1 slice (41 g) 135 Cal Banana cake 1 slice (45 g) 146 Cal
Fruit		
Strawberries, 1 cup (144 g) 46 Cal Orange, 1 small (96 g) 45 Cal Kiwi fruit, 1 medium (76 g) 46 Cal Prunes, 2 (16 g) 40 Cal Raisins, 1 Tbsp (10 g) 31 Cal	Banana, 1 small (100 g) 90 Cal Papaya, 1½ cups (210 g) 82 Cal Grapes, ½ cup (80 g) 55 Cal Pineapple, 1 cup (155 g) 75 Cal Mango, ½ cup (83 g) 54 Cal	Guava, 1 cup (165 g) 112 Cal Dried apricots, ½ cup (125 g) 106 Cal Pear, 1 medium (209 g) 121 Cal

Preparation time 15 minutes
Cooking time 20 minutes
Per serving 100 Cal

Ginger Melon Dessert

Even dieters need desserts. While many popular favourites are off the plan, fruit-based desserts are just as pleasurable.

Makes 4 servings

Water 2 cups (500 ml)

Sago pearls 4 Tbsp (60 g)

Rock melon 600 g, peeled, cut into cubes and chilled

Sugar 2 Tbsp

Lime juice 2 Tbsp (15 ml)

Soda water 1 cup (250 ml), chilled

Young ginger 20 g, peeled and sliced thinly

- Boil water in a pot. Add sago and cook until transparent. Drain, then plunge into cold water and drain again. Set aside.

- In a food processor, blend together rock melon and sugar, reserving a few cubes of rock melon as garnish.

- Mix together lime juice and soda water just before serving.

- To serve, portion rock melon puree into dessert bowls. Top with rock melon cubes, ginger and sago pearls.

- Garnish as desired. Serve as a dessert or snack.

Nutrition Fact

The 'sweet' note makes many healthier ingredients palatable, but use sugar wisely and in small amounts if you can spare the Calories. If you are still struggling to drop weight, you may want to replace the sugar with an artificial sweetener, so you can enjoy the sweet taste of dessert without the extra Calories.

Preparation time 8 minutes
Cooking time 40 minutes
Per serving 30 Cal (without added sugar)

White Fungus with Longan

Makes 4 servings

Dried white fungus 30 g

Dried longans 50 g

Red dates 20 g

Water 8 cups (2 litres)

Rock sugar to taste

- Soak white fungus in water until it expands. Wash thoroughly and shred loosely.

- Rinse longan and red dates.

- Boil the water in a large pot. Add all ingredients and boil for 30–40 minutes until fungus is soft. Add just enough rock sugar to sweeten the dessert.

- Serve warm as a dessert or snack.

Cooking Tip

Place all the ingredients into a slow cooker and set it to cook on low heat. When you get back after a day of work, you will be welcomed by this delicious dessert—all warm and comforting.

Nutrition Fact

Fungus is a great source of fibre. Add it to both sweet and savoury soups to enjoy the crunch.

1 Tbsp (13 g) rock sugar delivers 50 Cal. So watch how much you add to your recipe. Less is best.

Preparation time 5 minutes
Cooking time 45 minutes
Per serving 170 Cal

Barley Ginkgo Dessert

This nutritious dessert comes from the traditions of Chinese cuisine. It cleverly combines the wholesome barley grain with the ginkgo nut, which is believed to be health promoting.

Makes 4 servings

Water 8 cups (2 litres)

Barley 150 g

Ginkgo nuts 80 g

Dried bean curd sticks 50 g

Rock sugar to taste

- Boil the water in a large pot. Add barley and ginkgo nuts.
- Lower heat to medium and simmer for 30 minutes.
- Add bean curd sticks and sugar to taste. Let it boil for another 10–15 minutes.
- Serve warm as a dessert or snack.

Cooking Tip

Barley grains have a mild nutty flavour and chewy texture. Cook, drain and store refrigerated. Add to cooked rice, salads and soups to enhance the wholesomeness of your dishes.

Nutrition Fact

Barley is a mild flavoured whole grain that is a very good source of fibre and selenium. It is also a good source of minerals such as copper, magnesium and phosphorus.

Preparation time 10 minutes
Cooking time 5 minutes
Per serving 95 Cal

Banana & Strawberry Smoothie

Smoothies are easy to prepare. Pick sweet, seasonal fruit to blend up with milk or yoghurt. This refreshing blend makes a great breakfast drink or delicious snack..

Makes 4 servings

Bananas 2 (300 g), peeled

Strawberries 8 (180 g)

Low fat yoghurt 1¼ cups (300 g)

Alternative sweetener 4 Tbsp (5 g), optional

Ice cubes as needed

- Cut banana and strawberries into pieces.

- Place fruit, yoghurt and sweeterner in a blender and process until smooth.

- Portion into 4 glasses over ice cubes. Garnish as desired and serve immediately.

Cooking Tip

Bananas turn brown rather quickly once blended, so prepare this smoothie just a few minutes before you serve it.

Nutrition Fact

Juicing is an easy way to ensure that you take your daily servings of fruit. But remember, while juices are a nourishing choice, they do contain Calories. Overconsumption of fruit can tip the Calorie balance of a dieter.

Clockwise from top right: Banana and Strawberry Smoothie, Papaya and Banana Milkshake (page 164) and Mango Soy Smoothie (page 165)

Preparation time 10 minutes
Per serving 110 Cal

Papaya & Banana Milkshake

Local fruit are nutrient-dense, delivering loads of fibre, vitamin C and beta-carotene. This economical drink is a great way to start the day well nourished or to kill the craving for an unhealthy snack.

Makes 4 servings

Papaya cubes ¾ cup (105 g)

Banana 1 (120 g), peeled and cubed

Skim milk ¾ cup (180 ml)

Low fat plain yoghurt ¾ cup (180 ml)

Alternative sweetener 2 Tbsp (2.5 g), optional

Ice cubes as needed

• Place all ingredients, except ice cubes, in a blender and process until smooth.

• Portion into 4 glasses over ice cubes. Garnish as desired and serve immediately.

Cooking Tip

The sweetness of fresh fruit varies with the species and season, so taste the fruit shake before you decide to add the low Calorie alternative sweetener, if desired.

Nutrition Fact

Using lower fat dairy products (milk and yoghurt) helps to reduce the energy content of this fruity shake.

Preparation time 10 minutes
Per serving 110 Cal

Mango Soy Smoothie

Individuals with cow's milk sensitivity will appreciate this wholesome beverage. The glorious colour and rich consistency make this smoothie a pleasure to behold and drink.

Makes 4 servings

Mangoes 2 (400 g whole or 340 g edible portion), peeled, seed removed and cut into cubes

Soy milk 2 cups (500 ml)

Lemon juice 6 Tbsp (90 ml)

Alternative sweetener 2 Tbsp (2.5 g), optional

Ice cubes as needed

- Place all ingredients, except ice cubes, in a blender and process until smooth.

- Portion into 4 glasses over ice cubes. Garnish as desired and serve immediately.

Cooking Tip

Select ripe mangoes to prepare beverages as they are sweeter and easier to blend.

Nutrition Fact

Look for protein-rich, calcium-fortified, sugar-free soy milk as it delivers more nutritional value than the traditional soy milk sold in wet markets.

Preparation time 5 minutes
Per serving 20 Cal

Rosella Infusion

The calyces of the rosella plant, a species of hibiscus, is a perennial that grows abundantly in tropical countries like Indonesia, India, Africa, Mexico and the Caribbean islands, are brewed to prepare a brilliant pink, low Calorie tea-like infusion with a natural tangy flavour.

Makes 4 servings

Dried rosella flowers 16

Hot water 2 cups (500 ml)

Alternative sweetener 8 sachets (8 g)

Nata de coco cubes 4 Tbsp (80 g), optional

Ice cubes as needed

- Place rosella flowers and hot water in a large jug. Stir well and leave flower to steep in the water, for 10 minutes.

- Add alternate sweetener and stir well.

- Place equal portions of nata de coco into 4 tall glasses. Add some ice cubes. Top up with rosella infusion. Serve chilled.

Cooking Tip

Boiling the rosella calyces in hot water will lead to greater loss of vitamin C. Steeping in hot water conserves the fragile nutrient better.

Nutrition Fact

Rosella is believed to be a source of vitamin C and natural plant pigments called anthocyanins which are potent antioxidants.

Clockwise from top right: Rosella Infusion, Singapura Slim (page 168) and Cool Green Refresher (page 169)

Preparation time 10 minutes
Per serving 20 Cal

Singapura Slim

Inspired by Middle Eastern food traditions, this tangy refreshing low Calorie beverage is a great choice for constant hydration or a fancy party drink.

Makes 4 servings

Lemon juice 6 Tbsp (90 ml)

Mint leaves 12 (2 g)

Alternative sweetener 8 sachets (8 g)

Salt a pinch

Ice cubes as needed

Soda water 3⅕ cups (800 ml)

- Mix lemon juice, mint leaves, alternative sweetener and salt in a jug.

- Portion into 4 glasses filled with ice cubes.

- Top with soda water and serve chilled.

Cooking Tip

Mint leaves deliver intense aroma and flavor to pep up any sweet or savory dish. Use whole, minced or blended mint to brighten up the impact of beverages, salads, main dishes and desserts.

Nutrition Fact

Mint leaves are naturally low in Calories but a good source of vitamin A, C and folate.

Preparation time 10 minutes
Per serving 60 Cal

Cool Green Refresher

This tangy blend of fruit and vegetables is a low calorie beverage that presents a surprising fizz and flavor.

Makes 4 servings

Celery 1 stalk (140 g)

Cucumber 1 (300 g), soft centre cut out

Green apple 1 (100 g), cored

Lemon juice 2 Tbsp (30 ml)

Salt ½ tsp (3 g)

Soda water 1 can (330 ml), chilled

Ice cubes as needed

- Cut celery, cucumber and green apple into small pieces. Place in a juice extractor to extract the juice.

- Mix all juices with lemon juice, salt and soda. Pour into 4 glasses over ice cubes. Serve immediately.

Cooking Tip

The natural acidity in lemons helps to prevent the browning of the green apple juice. Retain the skin of the green apple to extract a more intensely colored juice.

Nutrition Fact

Soda water is also called carbonated water or seltzer. The fizz is created by adding carbon dioxide gas to water under pressure in a closed bottle. Once the can is opened, the gas rises to the surface and escapes.

Preparation time 10 minutes
Per serving 145 Cal

Kiwi, Pear & Celery Juice

Cool, green and refreshing, this pleasant combination of kiwi, celery and pear is designed to delight a slimmer's palate.

Makes 4 servings

Kiwi fruit 8, peeled and quartered

Green pears 2, cored and quartered

Celery 2 stalks

Salt a pinch

Soda water 3 cans (990 ml), chilled

Ice cubes as needed

- Place kiwi fruit, pears, celery and salt in a blender and blend until smooth.
- Mix with chilled soda water and portion into 4 glasses over ice cubes.

Cooking Tip

If you find peeling fruit fiddly, pick up cut slices from a fruit stall. This will make the preparation much easier.

Nutrition Fact

Whether you need to lose weight or not, you should aim to eat two servings of fruit every day. Fruit juices deliver vitamins, minerals and beneficial phytochemical but are almost devoid of fibre. Eat fruit when you can and remember that while fruit juice adds variety to the diet plan, a cup (250 ml) of pure fruit juice counts as a fruit serving.

Clockwise from top: Kiwi, Pear and Celery Juice, Orange Carrot Juice (page 172) and
Sweet Pineapple Ginger Juice (page 173)

Preparation time 10 minutes
Per serving 115 Cal

Sweet Pineapple Ginger Juice

Refreshing and tangy, this tropical juice will pep up your lower Calorie diet. Remember however that portion control is essential and do not over-indulge in this thirst quencher.

Makes 4 servings

Pineapple 880 g, peeled, cored and cut into cubes or about 4 wedges

Ginger 40 g, peeled and sliced

Lime juice 2 tsp (10 ml)

Ice cubes as needed

- Using a blender, extract pineapple and ginger juices.
- Mix together with lime juice.
- Portion into 4 glasses and serve chilled with ice.

Nutrition Fact

Juices are refreshing but deliver Calories in an easily consumable portion. So, make the pleasure last a while longer, serve the juice over ice. Not only will it taste better, the beverage will definitely fill you and hydrate you better.

Preparation time 10 minutes
Per serving 110 Cal

Orange Carrot Juice

Chock-full of vitamin C and beta carotene, this brilliant beverage will deliver on its promise to hydrate and nourish.

Makes 4 servings

Carrots 2, medium (400 g),
   cut into cubes

Oranges 2, large (600 g), peeled
   and quartered

Ground ginger a pinch

Ice cubes as needed

- Using a juice extractor, extract carrot and orange juices.

- Mix well with ground ginger.

- Portion into 4 glasses and serve chilled with ice.

Cooking Tip

Ginger acts as a foil to bring out the sweetness of the fruit. If you do not have ground ginger, extract ginger juice from fresh ginger by pounding or running the ginger through a blender.

Nutrition Fact

Many believe that detoxification is essential for weight loss and that drinking fruit or vegetable juices will help to detoxify the body. Most of us gain weight because we are consuming too many Calories and not exercising enough. It is definitely not about toxins and never expect to simply consume fruit or vegetable juices to detoxify your body and bring your weight down.

Appendix

	Breakfast	Lunch	Snack	Dinner	Calories
Day 1	High fibre white bread 2 slices (138 Cal) Reduced sugar jam 1 Tbsp (25 Cal) Skim milk 1 cup (86 Cal)	Oriental Fried Rice (page 80) 1 serving (340 Cal) Mango ½ cup (54 Cal)	Cool Green Refresher (page 169) 1 glass (60 Cal)	Steamed white rice 1 cup (240 Cal) Pork Rib and Lotus Root Soup (page 90) 1 serving (75 Cal) Spicy Sesame Salmon (page 108) 1 serving (180 Cal) Broccoli & Mushrooms in Sauce (page 134) 1 serving (60 Cal)	1258
	249	394	60	555	

	Breakfast	Lunch	Snack	Dinner	Calories
Day 2	Whole grain cereal ½ cup (106 Cal) Skim milk 1 cup (86 Cal) Raisins 1 Tbsp (31 Cal) Walnuts 1 Tbsp (49 Cal)	Seafood Tunghoon (page 72) 1 serving (320 Cal)	Singapura Slim (page 168) 1 glass (20 Cal) Steamed *soon kway* 1 piece (88 Cal)	Steamed white rice 1 cup (240 Cal) Tangy Assam Prawns (page 114) 1 serving (150 Cal) Stir-fried Long Beans with Squid (page 142) 1 serving (120 Cal) Kiwi 1, medium (46 Cal)	1256
	272	320	108	556	

	Breakfast	Lunch	Snack	Dinner	Calories
Day 3	Cornflakes, plain 1 cup (100 Cal) Low fat milk (2% fat) ½ cup (61 Cal) Banana 1, small (90 Cal) Almonds, sliced 1 Tbsp (33 Cal)	Nasi Briyani (page 82) 1 serving (500 Cal)	Pineapple 1 cup (75 Cal)	Steamed white rice 1 cup (240 Cal) Pan-fried Cod Fillet with Glazed Vegetables (page 112) 1 serving (150 Cal)	1249
	284	500	75	390	

	Breakfast	Lunch	Snack	Dinner	Calories
Day 4	Mushroom & Cheese Toast (page 46) 1 serving (100 Cal) Reduced sugar high calcium soy milk 1 cup (143 Cal)	Char Kway Teow (page 70) 1 serving (330 Cal) Fresh guava 1 cup (112 Cal)	Papaya & Banana Milkshake (page 164) 1 glass (110 Cal)	Carrot Soup (page 92) 1 serving (90 Cal) Hamburger bun 1 bun (164 Cal) Mini Chicken Patties (page 118) 1 serving (140 Cal) Iceberg lettuce 2 leaves (2 Cal) Watermelon Salad (page 98) 1 serving (55 Cal)	**1246**
	243	442	110	451	

	Breakfast	Lunch	Snack	Dinner	Calories
Day 5	Egg Omelette Wrap (page 58) 1 serving (160 Cal) Wholemeal bread 1 slice (73 Cal) Skim milk 1 cup (86 Cal)	Macaroni & Chicken Soup (page 66) 1 serving (290 Cal) Apple 1, small (77 Cal)	Sweet Pineapple Ginger Juice (page 172) 1 glass (115 Cal)	Steamed white rice 1 cup (240 Cal) Baked Whole Trevally (page 104) 1 serving (120 Cal) Steamed Aubergines (page 146) 1 serving (90 Cal)	**1251**
	319	367	115	450	

	Breakfast	Lunch	Snack	Dinner	Calories
Day 6	Oatmeal Porridge (page 44) 1 serving (150 Cal) Skim milk 1 cup (86 Cal)	Curry Noodles (page 68) 1 serving (490 Cal)	Rosella Infusion (page 166) 1 glass (20 Cal) Honeydew 1 cup (61 Cal)	Steamed white rice 1 cup (240 Cal) Easy Sardines (page 102) 1 serving (200 Cal) Xiao Bai Cai in Broth (page 140) 1 serving (25 Cal)	**1272**
	236	490	81	465	

	Breakfast	Lunch	Snack	Dinner	Calories
Day 7	Tuna Pita Pizza (page 48) 1 serving (155 Cal) Banana 1 small (90 Cal) Tea, plain 1 cup (0 Cal)	Chicken Breast with Spicy Mango Salad (page 116) 1 serving (100 Cal) Steamed white rice 1 cup (240 Cal)	Banana & Strawberry Smoothie (page 162) 1 glass (95 Cal)	Steamed white rice 1 cup (240 Cal) Pan-fried Firm Tofu (page 130) 1 serving (240 Cal)	**1160**
	245	340	95	480	

	Breakfast	Lunch	Snack	Dinner	Calories
Day 1	Wholemeal bread 2 slices (146 Cal) Mayonnaise, light 1 Tbsp (49 Cal) Turkey ham, extra lean 1 slice (24 Cal) Iceberg lettuce 1 leaf (1 Cal) Black coffee 1 cup (0 Cal)	Chicken Rice (page 78) 1 serving (460 Cal) Strawberries 1 cup (46 Cal)	Orange Carrot Juice (page 173) 1 glass (110 Cal)	Steamed white rice 1 cup (240 Cal) Chicken & Melon Soup (page 88) 1 serving (20 Cal) Sweet & Sour Pork (page 124) 1 serving (230 Cal) Stir-fried Kailan (page 138) 1 serving (90 Cal)	1416
	220	506	110	580	

	Breakfast	Lunch	Snack	Dinner	Calories
Day 2	Soft-boiled Egg (page 38) 1 serving (71 Cal) Whitemeal bread 1 slice (73 Cal) Reduced sugar baked beans ¼ can (88 Cal) Skim milk 1 glass (86 Cal)	Glutinous Rice (page 64) 1 serving (400 Cal) Papaya 1½ cups (82 Cal)	Pandan chiffon cake 1 slice (135 Cal) Black coffee 1 cup (0 Cal)	Steamed white rice 1 cup (240 Cal) Steamed Sea Bass (page 106) 1 serving (170 Cal) Xiao Bai Chye in Broth (page 140) 1 serving (25 Cal) Pear ½, medium (61 Cal)	1431
	318	482	135	496	

	Breakfast	Lunch	Snack	Dinner	Calories
Day 3	Fish Porridge (page 50) 1 serving (190 Cal) Dried prunes 3 (60 Cal)	Nasi Lemak (page 74) 1 serving (525 Cal) Orange 1, small (45 Cal)	Mango Soy Smoothie (page 165) 1 glass (110 Cal)	Steamed white rice 1 cup (240 Cal) Beef Stew (page 126) 1 serving (250 Cal) Spinach with Eggs (page 136) 1 serving (80 Cal)	1500
	250	570	110	570	

	Breakfast	Lunch	Snack	Dinner	Calories
Day 4	Fat-free Chapatti (page 54) 1 serving (165 Cal) Lentil & Vegetables (page 56) 1 serving (105 Cal) Apple 1, small (77 Cal) Low fat milk (2% fat) 1 cup (122 Cal)	Japanese Cold Noodles (page 52) 1 serving (190 Cal) Japanese Cold Tofu (page 130) 1 serving (30 Cal) Persimmon 1 (118 Cal)	Barley Ginkgo Dessert (page 160) 1 serving (170 Cal)	Steamed white rice 1 cup (240 Cal) Ngoh Hiang (page 150) 1 serving (205 Cal) Stir-fried Ladies Fingers (page 148) 1 serving (70 Cal)	1492
	469	338	170	515	

	Breakfast	Lunch	Snack	Dinner	Calories
Day 5	Cornflakes, plain 1 cup (100 Cal) Low fat milk (2% fat) ½ cup (61 Cal) Banana 1 small (90 Cal) Sliced almonds 1 Tbsp (33 Cal)	Vegetable Pulao (page 76) 1 serving (290 Cal) Papaya Banana Milkshake (page 164) 1 serving (110 Cal)	White Fungus with Longan (page 158) 1 serving (30 Cal) Vegetable *pau* 1 whole (150 Cal)	Steamed white rice 1 cup (240 Cal) Salmon & Vegetable Parcel (page 110) 1 serving (200 Cal) Carrot Soup (page 92) 1 serving (90 Cal) Plums 2, small (60 Cal)	**1454**
	284	400	180	590	

	Breakfast	Lunch	Snack	Dinner	Calories
Day 6	Wholemeal bread 2 slices (146 Cal) Mayonnaise, light 1 Tbsp (49 Cal) Turkey ham, extra lean 1 slice (24 Cal) Lettuce leaf 1 leaf (1 Cal) Black coffee 1 cup (0 Cal) Low fat milk (2% fat) 1 cup (122 Cal)	Wonton with spinach noodles, dry 1 serving (480 Cal) Papaya 1 wedge (55 Cal)	Plain *chee cheong fun* with sauce 1 serving (133 Cal)	Steamed white rice 1 cup (240 Cal) Spicy Chicken with Cashew Nuts (page 120) 1 serving (160 Cal) Citrus Pomelo (page 96) 1 serving (105 Cal)	**1515**
	342	535	133	505	

	Breakfast	Lunch	Snack	Dinner	Calories
Day 7	Basic Omelette (page 39) 1 serving (71 Cal) High fibre white bread 2 slices (138 Cal) Tomato, grilled 1 small (15 Cal) Mushrooms, grilled ¼ cup (4 Cal) Non-fat fruit yoghurt 1 cup (233 Cal)	Macaroni & Chicken Soup (page 66) 1 serving (290 Cal) Barley water 1 glass (55 Cal)	Watermelon Salad (page 98) 1 serving (55 Cal) Banana cake 1 slice (146 Cal)	Steamed white rice 1 cup (240 Cal) Roast Lean Pork (page 122) 1 serving (130 Cal) Steamed Pumpkin with Wolfberries (page 144) 1 serving (40 Cal) Pork Rib & Lotus Root Soup (page 90) 1 serving (75 Cal)	**1492**
	461	345	201	485	

Calorie Expenditure Table

Activity	Calories Per Minute			
	50 kg	60 kg	70 kg	80 kg
Running (8 km/h)	7	8.5	10	11
Running (9.6 km/h)	9	10.5	12	14
Running (11.2 km/h)	10	12	14	16
Running (12.8 km/h)	12	14	16.5	19
Strolling/leisure walking	3	3.5	4	5
Badminton	4	5	5.5	6
Table tennis	3.5	4	5	5.5
Tennis	6	7	8.5	10
Golf	4	5	5.5	6
Tai chi	3.5	4	5	5.5
Roller blading	11	13	15	18
Skateboarding	4	5	6	7
Trampoline	3	3.5	4	5
Leisure swimming	5	6	7	8
Snorkeling	4	5	6	7
Canoeing (light effort)	2.5	3	3.5	4
Canoeing (moderate effort)	6	7	8.5	10
Canoeing (vigorous effort)	10.5	12.5	15	17
Sailing	2.5	3	3.5	4

Reference: Ainsworth B.E. et al. *Compendium of Physical Activities: An Update of Activity Codes and MET Intensities, Med Sci Sports Exerc.* 2000, 32: S498-504.

Additional Reading Materials

Books & Pamphlets

Health Promotion Board, Singapore

ABCs of Healthy Eating

Choosing Food? Read The Label

Dietary Guideline 2003 for Adult Singaporeans (18–65 years)

Fat Matters

American Dietetic Association

Eat Right for a Healthy Weight

Healthy Eating on the Run

Shop Smart

Get the Facts on Food Labels

Smart Snacking for Adults and Teens

Step Up to Nutrition and Health

References

American Dietetic Association
http://www.eatright.org

Asian Food Information Centre
http://www.afic.org/

Center for Disease Control
http://www.cdc.gov/

Health Promotion Board
http://www.hpb.gov.sg

Mayo Clinic
http://www.mayoclinic.org/

WebMD
http://www.webmd.com/

World Health Organization
http://www.who.int/en/

Resources

NutriBase Clinical Nutrition Manager, v7.17

Nutrient Data Laboratories, USDA National Nutrient Database for Standard Reference

Food Info Search, Health Promotion Board, Singapore

NutriWEB Malaysia, Malaysian Food Composition Database

About the Authors

Anna Jacob is a nutritionist and dietitian with over 26 years of experience in Singapore. She is currently the Nutrition Science and Communications Manager of Abbott Nutrition International, a division of Abbott Laboratories (Singapore) Private Limited. Anna is also a Board Member of the Singapore Heart Foundation and a Member of the Asia Research and Development Team of Abbott Nutrition Research and Development Centre, Biopolis, Singapore.

Anna earned a bachelor's degree in Nutrition and Dietetics and master's degree in Food Service Management and Dietetics from the Women's Christian College, Madras, India. She is also a full member of the Singapore Nutrition and Dietetics Association (SNDA), the local professional organization in which she has held the posts of Editor and President.

Prior to joining Abbott, she was a founding partner and Director of Food and Nutrition Specialists P L, a nutrition consultancy firm set up in Singapore since 1989. Through this period, she also served as the Associate Director, Scientific Programs for the International Life Sciences Institute Southeast Asia Region (ILSI SEAR).

Anna is a co-author of *FirstFoods* and *SmartFoods for Tweens*, published by Marshall Cavendish International (Asia) Pte Ltd.

Ng Hooi Lin is curently employed as the Nutritionist at Singapore Heart Foundation. She is also a full member of the Singapore Nutrition and Dietetic Association (SNDA) and holds a Bachelor of Science in Nutrition and a Master in Sports Science.

She has a particular interest in community health promotion and is actively involved in planning and implementing community educational programmes in the areas of heart health and nutrition.

Hooi Lin also plays an active role in supporting health promotion programmes in schools to help students cultivate healthy eating habits.

Hooi Lin contributes articles regularly to several magazines, newspaper and websites, including *Health No. 1, Lianhe Zaobao* and omy.sg (online mobile for the young). She also maintains an active online presence via her personal blog (http://nghooilin.blogspot.com).

Hooi Lin co-authored *SmartFoods for Tweens* with Anna.

More about the Book

For more about the story behind the scenes of this book or to chat with the authors, visit http://fitnotfatasia.blogspot.com